How Languages are Learned

Also published in
Oxford Handbooks for Language Teachers

Teaching English Overseas: An Introduction
Sandra Lee McKay

Teaching American English Pronunciation
Peter Avery and Susan Ehrlich

Teaching Business English
Mark Ellis and Christine Johnson

Communication in the Language Classroom
Tony Lynch

How Languages are Learned

Patsy M. Lightbown and Nina Spada

In collaboration with
Leila Ranta and Jude Rand

Oxford University Press

Oxford University Press
Walton Street, Oxford OX2 6DP

Oxford New York
Athens Auckland Bangkok Bombay
Calcutta Cape Town Dar es Salaam Delhi
Florence Hong Kong Istanbul Karachi
Kuala Lumpur Madras Madrid Melbourne
Mexico City Nairobi Paris Singapore
Taipei Tokyo Toronto

and associated companies in
Berlin Ibadan

Oxford and *Oxford English*
are trade marks of Oxford University Press.

ISBN 0 19 437169 7

Set in Adobe Garamond
by Tradespools Ltd., Frome, Somerset
Printed in Hong Kong

To our parents, with love and gratitude

CONTENTS

Acknowledgements xi
Introduction xiii

1 **Learning a first language** 1
Say what I say: the behaviourist position 1
It's all in your mind: the innatist position 7
 The 'critical period' hypothesis 11
Mom's the word: the interactionist position 13
 Caretaker talk 14
Summary 16

2 **Theories of second language learning** 19
 Activity: Learner profiles 20
Behaviourism: the second language view 23
Cognitive theory: a new psychological approach 25
Creative construction theory 26
 1 The acquisition-learning hypothesis 26
 2 The monitor hypothesis 27
 3 The natural order hypothesis 27
 4 The input hypothesis 28
 5 The affective filter hypothesis 28
 Summary 29
The second language interactionist view 29
Summary 30

3 **Factors affecting second language learning** 33
 Activity: Characteristics of the 'good language learner' 33
Research on learner characteristics 35
 Intelligence 36
 Aptitude 37
 Personality 38
 Motivation and attitudes 39
 Learning styles 40
 Age of acquisition 41
Summary 50

4 **Learner language**   53

The concept of learner language   54
  Activity: The Great Toy Robbery   55
Developmental sequences   57
  Grammatical morphemes   57
  Negative sentences   59
  Question formation   61
  Activity: Learners' questions   64
  Relative Clauses   65
More about sequences of development   66
Summary   67

5 **Second language learning in the classroom**   69

Comparing instructed and natural settings for language learning 69
  Activity: Natural and instructional settings   69
  Activity: Classroom comparisons   73
Five proposals for classroom teaching   78
  1 Get it right from the beginning   79
  2 Say what you mean and mean what you say   83
  3 Just listen   88
  4 Teach what is teachable   92
  5 Get it right in the end   96
The implications of classroom research for teaching   103
Summary   105

6 **Popular ideas about language learning: Facts and opinions** 111

  1 Languages are learned mainly through imitation   111
  2 Parents usually correct young children when they make
     grammatical errors   112
  3 People with high IQs are good language learners   112
  4 The most important factor in second language acquisition
     success is motivation   112
  5 The earlier a second language is introduced in school
     programs, the greater the likelihood of success in learning 112
  6 Most of the mistakes second language learners make are
     due to interference from their first language   113
  7 Teachers should present grammatical rules one at a time, and
     learners should practise examples of each one before going
     on to another   113
  8 Teachers should teach simple language structures before
     complex ones   114
  9 Learners' errors should be corrected as soon as they are made
     in order to prevent the formation of bad habits   114

10 Teachers should use materials that expose students only to
    those language structures which they have already been
    taught   115
11 When learners are allowed to interact freely they learn each
    others' mistakes   115
12 Students learn what they are taught   116
Conclusion   116

Glossary   119
Bibliography   127
Index   133

ACKNOWLEDGEMENTS

This book arises from fifteen years of friendship and professional collaboration during which we have worked—both separately and together—in classroom centered research on second language acquisition. We have both taught language acquisition courses in university teacher training programs and in courses for in-service teachers. We have developed our ideas about the relationship between language acquisition research and classroom practice as we have interacted with these new and experienced teachers. In 1989, with the help of Jude Rand, we produced, for the Ministère de l'Éducation du Québec, a set of materials for use in workshops for experienced ESL teachers in primary and secondary schools in Quebec. The teachers' and workshop leaders' response to these materials was very positive. They expressed their feeling that this opportunity to know more about language acquisition was an important part of their professional development. Paul Meara read these materials and encouraged us to write a book for other second and foreign language teachers. It was he who put us in contact with the wonderful team at Oxford University Press whose support and patience have been invaluable in helping us see the book through to completion. Throughout the writing of the book, we were assisted in a thousand ways by Leila Ranta. We are very grateful to colleagues and friends in Canada and abroad whose enthusiasm for earlier versions of the book gave us the courage to keep working on it.

The publishers and authors thank the publishers of *Language Learning* for permission to reproduce the figure by Mark Patkowski.

Every effort has been made to trace the owners of copyright material in this book, but we should be pleased to hear from any copyright holder whom we have been unable to contact. We apologize for any apparent negligence. If notified, the publisher will be pleased to rectify any errors or omissions at the earliest opportunity.

Cartoons by Sophie Grillet © Oxford University Press 1993.

INTRODUCTION

Every few years, new foreign language teaching methods arrive on the scene. New textbooks appear far more frequently. They are usually proclaimed to be more effective than those that have gone before, and, in many cases, these methods or textbooks are promoted or even prescribed for immediate use. New methods and textbooks may reflect current developments in linguistic/ applied linguistic theory or recent pedagogical trends. Sometimes they are said to be based on recent developments in language acquisition theory and research. For example, one approach to teaching may emphasize the value of having students imitate and practise a set of correct sentences while another emphasizes the importance of encouraging 'natural' communication be-tween learners. How is a teacher to evaluate the potential effectiveness of new methods? One important basis for evaluating is, of course, the teacher's own experience with previous successes or disappointments. In addition, teachers who are informed about some of the findings of recent research are better prepared to judge whether the new proposals for language teaching are likely to bring about positive changes in students' learning.

This book is about how languages are learned. It has been written for second and foreign language teachers. We believe that information about findings and theoretical views in second language acquisition research can make you a better judge of claims made by textbook writers and proponents of various language teaching methods. Such information, combined with insights gained from your experience as a language teacher or learner, can help you evaluate proposed changes in classroom methodology.

Before we begin . . .

Take a moment to reflect on your views about how languages are learned and what the implications are for how they should be taught. Below are twelve popular views about language learning. Think about whether you agree or disagree with some of these views.

In the last chapter of this book, we will return to these popular views and examine them in the light of the research on language learning which is discussed in Chapters 1–5.

The book begins with a chapter on how children learn their first language. Both second language research and second language teaching have been influenced by theories of how children acquire their first language. In fact, one of the significant findings of second language acquisition research has been that there are important similarities between first and second language acquisition. In Chapter 2, several theories which have been proposed to account for second language learning are presented and assessed. Some of the questions raised in Chapters 1 and 2 include: Is language learning just like any other kind of learning? Is there a biologically determined age limit for first language acquisition? How important are imitation and practice for language learning? Does it help to correct learners when they make errors? To what extent can theories of learning a first language be applied to second language learning?

In Chapter 3, we turn our attention to how individual learner characteristics and different contexts for second language learning may affect success. The discussion includes issues such as the importance of learners' attitudes toward the second language and the possibility that there is a special aptitude for language learning. The question of how the learner's age affects success in second language learning is also discussed.

In Chapter 4, we review some of the research findings about second language learners' changing knowledge of the language and their ability to use that knowledge. We look at interpretations of learners' errors and at the characteristics of learners' language at different stages of development for first and second language learners.

Chapter 5 begins with a comparison of natural and instructional environments for second language learning. The chapter focuses on five proposals for the most effective way to teach second languages. Findings from research in second language classrooms are presented and discussed.

In Chapter 6, as noted above, popular views about language learning and teaching are critically examined and revised in light of current research.

A Glossary provides a quick reference for a number of terms which may be new or which have specific technical meanings in the context of language acquisition research. Glossary words are italicized where they first appear in the text. For readers who would like to have more detailed information about some of the research, a list of sources and further readings is included at the end of each chapter, and a Bibliography at the end of the book.

We have tried to present the information in a way which does not require readers to be familiar with research methods or theoretical issues. Each chapter summarizes important developments in first and/or second language acquisition research and theory. Examples and case studies are included throughout the book to illustrate the research ideas. Many of the examples are taken from second language classrooms.

1 Languages are learned mainly through imitation.

strongly agree ___|___|___|___|___|___ strongly disagree

2 Parents usually correct young children when they make grammatical errors.

strongly agree ___|___|___|___|___|___ strongly disagree

3 People with high IQs are good language learners.

strongly agree ___|___|___|___|___|___ strongly disagree

4 The most important factor in second language acquisition success is motivation.

strongly agree ___|___|___|___|___|___ strongly disagree

5 The earlier a second language is introduced in school programs, the greater the likelihood of success in learning.

strongly agree ___|___|___|___|___|___ strongly disagree

6 Most of the mistakes which second language learners make are due to interference from their first language.

strongly agree ___|___|___|___|___|___ strongly disagree

7 Teachers should present grammatical rules one at a time, and learners should practise examples of each one before going on to another.

strongly agree ___|___|___|___|___|___ strongly disagree

8 Teachers should teach simple language structures before complex ones.

strongly agree ___|___|___|___|___|___ strongly disagree

9 Learners' errors should be corrected as soon as they are made in order to prevent the formation of bad habits.

strongly agree ___|___|___|___|___|___ strongly disagree

10 Teachers should use materials that expose students only to those language structures which they have already been taught.

strongly agree ___|___|___|___|___|___ strongly disagree

11 When learners are allowed to interact freely (for example in group or pair activities), they learn each others' mistakes.

strongly agree ___|___|___|___|___|___ strongly disagree

12 Students learn what they are taught.

strongly agree ___|___|___|___|___|___ strongly disagree

1 LEARNING A FIRST LANGUAGE

One of the most fascinating aspects of human development is the ability to learn language. We all watch and listen with absolute fascination as the first 'coos' and 'gurgles', sounding very much like conversation, are uttered by a six-month-old baby. We all share in the pride and joy of parents whose one-year-old has uttered the first 'bye bye'. Indeed, learning a language is an amazing feat—one which has attracted the attention of linguists and psychologists for generations. How do children accomplish this? What is it that enables a child not only to learn words, but to put them together in meaningful sentences? What pushes children to go on developing complex grammatical language even though their early simple communication is successful for most purposes?

In this chapter, we will consider several theories which have been offered as explanations of how language is learned. Three central theoretical positions will be discussed in turn: the behaviourist, the innatist, and the interactionist views of *language acquisition*. Each section will involve a case study to illustrate the phenomenon under discussion.

Say what I say: the behaviourist position

Traditional *behaviourists* believed that *language learning* is simply a matter of imitation and habit formation. Children imitate the sounds and patterns which they hear around them and receive positive reinforcement (which could take the form of praise or just successful communication) for doing so. Thus encouraged by their environment, they continue to imitate and practise these sounds and patterns until they form 'habits' of correct language use. According to this view, the quality and quantity of the language which the child hears, as well as the consistency of the reinforcement offered by others in the environment, should have an effect on the child's success in language learning.

The behaviourist view of how language is learned has an intuitive appeal. And there is no doubt that it can offer a partial explanation of children's early language learning. However, it is useful to examine actual language data to see how well this view accounts for the development of some more complex aspects of their language.

The behaviourists view *imitation* and *practice* as primary processes in language development. To clarify what is meant by these two terms, consider the following definitions and examples.

Imitation: Word for word repetition of all or part of someone else's utterance.

> **Mother** Would you like some bread and peanut butter?
> **Katie**   Some bread and peanut butter.

Practice: Repetitive manipulation of form.

> **Michel** I can handle it. Hannah can handle it. We can handle it.

Activity

Analysing children's speech

Examine these transcripts from Peter, Cindy, and Kathryn, who are about the same age. The transcripts are based on recordings made while the children were playing with a visiting adult.

Transcription conventions:

> XXX = incomprehensible speech
> ... = pause
> parentheses = description of non-verbal events

Peter (24 months)
(Peter is playing with a dump truck while two adults look on.)

> Peter (finding a car) Get more.
> Lois You're gonna put more wheels in the dump truck?
> Peter Dump truck. Wheels. Dump truck.

(later)

> Patsy What happened to it (the truck)?
> Peter (looking under chair for it) Lose it. Dump truck! Dump truck!
>   Fall! Fall!
> Lois Yes, the dump truck fell down.
> Peter Dump truck fell down. Dump truck.

Peter (25 months)
(Peter, Patsy, and Lois are playing with pencil and paper.)

> Peter (indicating he wants Patsy to draw) Lois. Lois too. Patsy.
>   Lois too!
> Patsy You want me to make a car? OK.

(Patsy draws a tiny car like Lois's.)

> Patsy Oh, you want Lois to have some paper?
> Peter Lois have some paper?

(later)

> Patsy Let's see if I can draw what you draw. Draw something!
> Peter Draw something!

(Unpublished data from P. M. Lightbown.)

It is easy to see that Peter imitates a great deal. However, it should be stressed that very few children imitate to the extent that Peter does. Thirty to forty per cent of Peter's speech consists of imitations while, for some children, the rate of imitation may be less than ten per cent.

It is also important to note that his imitations are not random; he doesn't imitate everything he hears. Very detailed analyses showed that Peter imitates new words and sentence structures until they become solidly grounded in his language system, and then he stops imitating these and goes on to imitate other new words and structures. Thus, unlike a parrot who imitates the familiar and continues to repeat the same things again and again, children's imitation is selective and based on what they are currently learning. In other words, even when the child imitates, the choice of what to imitate seems to be based on something the child already knows, not simply on what is 'available' in the environment.

Cindy (24 months, 16 days)
(Cindy is looking at a picture of a carrot in a book and trying to get Patsy's attention.)

> **Cindy** Kawo? kawo? kawo? kawo? kawo?
> **Patsy** What are the rabbits eating?
> **Cindy** They eating ... kando?
> **Patsy** No, that's a carrot.
> **Cindy** Carrot. (pointing to each carrot on the page) The other ... carrot. The other carrot. The other carrot.

(A few minutes later, Cindy brings Patsy a stuffed toy rabbit.)

> **Patsy** What does this rabbit like to eat?
> **Cindy** (xxx) eat the carrots.

(Cindy gets another stuffed rabbit.)

> **Cindy** He (xxx) eat carrots. The other one eat carrots. They both eat carrots.

(One week later, Cindy opens the book to the same page.)

> **Cindy** Here's the carrots. (pointing) Is that a carrot?
> **Patsy** Yes.

Cindy (25 months, 1 day)

> **Cindy** (playing with several dolls, one of which she calls a 'tiger') Doll go to sleep.
> **Patsy** Does the doll want to go to sleep?
> **Cindy** (not answering Patsy, but talking to dolls in 'motherly' tones) Okay, I take you. Come on, Doll ... (xxx). Go to sleep with the tiger (xxx) go to sleep. Doll wants to go to sleep.
> **Patsy** Does the tiger want to go to sleep?
> **Cindy** Tiger wants to go to sleep. The doll wants to go to sleep. He go to sleep.

(Unpublished data from P. M. Lightbown.)

Cindy appears to be working hard on her language acquisition. She practises new structures in a way that sometimes makes her sound like a student in a foreign language classroom! Her 'He eat carrots. The other one eat carrots. They both eat carrots' is reminiscent of a *substitution drill*. However, again it should be stressed that not all children 'practise' to the extent that Cindy does in these examples, and Cindy herself is practising more here than in some other samples of her speech.

The samples of speech from Peter and Cindy would seem to lend some support to the behaviourist explanation of language acquisition. But such imitation and practice do not account for how these children learn all aspects of their native language. Furthermore, we also need to account for the normal language development of children who rarely imitate and practise in the way that Peter and Cindy do in these examples. Look at the following conversation between Kathryn and Lois. Who is in charge of this conversation?

Kathryn (24 months)

Lois	Did you see the toys I brought?
Kathryn	I bring toys? Choo choo? Lois brought the choo choo train?
Lois	Yes, Lois brought the choo choo train.
Kathryn	(reaching for bag) I want play with choo choo train. I want play with choo choo train. (taking out slide) Want play. What's this?
Lois	Oh you know what that is.
Kathryn	Put down on floor. This. I do this.

(Kathryn puts the slide on the floor.)

Kathryn	(taking out two cars of train) Do this. I want do this. (trying to put train together) I do this. I do this.
Lois	OK. You can do it. You can do it. Look I'll show you how.

(Lois puts it together.)

Kathryn	(searching in box) I get a more. Get a more. No more choo choo train. Get truck. (taking out truck) Kathryn truck. Where? Where a more choo choo train?
Lois	Inside. It's in the box.
Kathryn	A choo choo? (taking out part of train) This a choo choo train.

(Bloom and Lahey 1978)

Like Cindy, Kathryn sometimes repeats herself but rarely imitates the other speaker. Instead, she answers questions or poses them. She also elaborates on the other speaker's questions or statements. She is very much in charge of the conversation and the activity here!

Other children

Look at the following examples taken from various children in which imitation does not appear to be involved. Think about how the children arrive at the forms they produce. (These examples are from unpublished data collected by P. M. Lightbown and J. Rand.)

(Note: The ages of children are shown in years and months: for example, 6,10 means six years and ten months.)

1	**Kyo** (6,10)	I'm hungry.
	Dad	We'll have some poppy seed bread in a little while.
	Kyo	No. I want it now.
	Dad	We have to wait 'til it's defrosted.
	Kyo	But I like it *frossed*.

2 Randall (3,0) had a little bump on his hand and his mother said that they'd have to take him to the doctor.

> **Randall**   Why? So he can *doc* my little bump?

3   **Michel** (2,10)   Mummy, I'm *hiccing up* and I can't stop.

4   **Mother**   Get undressed (after many repetitions)
       David (3,11)   I'm getting undressed.
                           I'm getting *on dressed.*
                           I'm getting on dressed.
                           I'm getting *off dressed.*

Numbers 1 to 4 are all examples of children in the process of learning the rules of word formation and *overgeneralizing* them to new contexts.

(1) Kyo recognizes the prefix *de-* as negating the root word so his version of the opposite of 'defrosted' comes out as 'frossed'.
(2) Randall forms the verb 'doc' from the noun 'doctor', by analogy with farmers who farm, swimmers who swim, and actors who act.
(3) Michel has heard many two-word verbs with *up*, such as 'stand up' and 'pick up'. On that basis, his generalization is perfectly sensible.
(4) David isn't sure what he hears. He doesn't yet understand the prefix *un-*. He first analyses the sounds and concludes that it is 'on dressed'. Then he analyses the situation and concludes that this time he's supposed to be taking things *off* and so he arrives at the conclusion that he should be getting 'off dressed', not 'on dressed'.

5   At Lucy's twelfth birthday party, toasts were proposed with grape juice in stemmed glasses:

> **Father**   I'd like to propose a toast.

After a long period without toasts, David (5,l) raised his glass and said 'I'd like to propose a piece of bread.' Only after all the laughter sent David slinking from the table did the group realize that he wasn't joking!

6   **Mother**   I love you to pieces.
       David (4,1) I love you *three* pieces.

Numbers 5 and 6 are examples of creative use of vocabulary. In each case the child is in the process of discovering the full (or limited) meaning of the word in question.

(5) David is fascinated by the ritual language which accompanies this strange new event of lifting glasses. He is concentrating so hard on the gesture and the *formulaic* expression 'I'd like to propose . . .' that he fails to realize that the word he already knows—toast—is not the same toast and can't be replaced with a phrase which is its near-synonym in other contexts—a piece of bread.

(6) What does 'to pieces' mean anyway? At least *two* pieces would give some indication of how much she loves me! And I can do better than that! Three pieces!

7   **Randall** (2,9)   Are dogs can wiggle their tails?

8   **Randall** (3,5)   You took all the towels away because I can't dry my hands.

Numbers 7 and 8 are both examples of systematic misuse of basic sentence construction which has not been fully acquired.

(7) He has begun to ask correct yes/no questions. This means placing the auxiliary verb at the beginning of the sentence. Randall has misinterpreted the rule and concluded that the trick of asking questions is to put a certain word at the beginning of the sentence—somewhat like the French *est-ce que* form. Other examples include 'Are those are my boots?' and 'Are this is hot?'

(8) He means 'I can't dry my hands because you took all the towels away'. He has made a mistake about which clause comes first. Children at this age tend to state events in the order of their occurrence. In this case, the towels disappeared before he attempted to dry his hands.

Errors such as these provide us with a window on to the process of language learning. Imitation and practice alone cannot explain such errors since the forms created by the child were never produced by adults. Rather, children appear to pick out patterns and then generalize them to new contexts. They create new forms or new uses of words until they finally figure out how the forms are used by adults.

The behaviourist explanations for language acquisition offer a reasonable way of understanding how children learn some of the regular and routine aspects of language. However, their acquisition of the more complex grammatical structures of the language requires a different sort of explanation and we will see below some of the proposals for going beyond the behaviourist view.

It's all in your mind: the innatist position

The linguist Noam Chomsky claims that children are biologically programmed for language and that language develops in the child in just the same way that other biological functions develop. For example, every child will learn to walk as long as adequate nourishment and reasonable freedom of movement are provided. The child does not have to be taught; most children learn to walk at about the same time; and walking is essentially the same in all normal human beings. For Chomsky, language acquisition is very

similar to the development of walking. The environment makes a basic contribution—in this case, the availability of people who speak to the child. The
child, or rather, the child's biological endowment, will do the rest. This is
known as the *innatist* position. Chomsky developed his theory in reaction to
the behaviourist theory of learning based on imitation and habit formation
(Chomsky 1959).

Chomsky argues that the behaviourist theory fails to recognize what has
come to be called 'the logical problem of language acquisition'. This logical
problem refers to the fact that children come to know more about the structure of their language than they could reasonably be expected to learn on the
basis of the samples of language which they hear. According to Chomsky,
the language the child is exposed to in the environment is full of confusing
information (for example, false starts, incomplete sentences, or slips of the
tongue) and does not provide all the information which the child needs.
Furthermore, the evidence seems very strong that children are by no means
systematically corrected or instructed on language points. Parental corrections have been observed to be inconsistent or even non-existent. When
parents do correct, they tend to focus on meaning and not on language itself.
According to Chomsky, children's minds are not blank slates to be filled
merely by imitating language they hear in the environment. Instead he
claims that children are born with a special ability to discover for themselves
the underlying rules of a language system.

Chomsky originally referred to this special ability as being based on a *language acquisition device* (LAD). This device was often described as an imaginary 'black box' which exists somewhere in the brain. This 'black box', which
is thought to contain all and *only* the principles which are universal to all human languages, prevents the child from going off on lots of wrong trails in
trying to discover the rules of the language. For the LAD to work, the child
needs access only to samples of the natural language. These language samples serve as a trigger to activate the device. Once it is activated, the child is
able to discover the structure of the language to be learned by matching the
innate knowledge of basic grammatical relationships to the structures of the
particular language in the environment. In recent writings, Chomsky and
his followers no longer use the term LAD, but refer to the child's innate endowment as *Universal Grammar* (UG). UG is considered to consist of a set of
principles which are common to all languages. If children are pre-equipped
with UG, then what they have to learn is the ways in which their own language makes use of these principles and the variations on those principles
which may exist in the particular language they are learning (Chomsky
1981, Cook 1988, White 1989).

Chomsky drew attention to the fact that children seem to develop language
in similar ways and on a similar schedule, in a way not very different from

the way all children learn to walk. Environmental differences may be associated with some variation in the rate of acquisition (how quickly children learn), but adult linguistic competence (the knowledge of how their language works) is very similar for all speakers of one language. In acquiring the intricate and complex systems that make up a language, young children, whose abilities are fairly limited in many ways, accomplish, with apparent ease, something which adult *second language* learners may envy.

Here is a summary of the kinds of evidence which have been used to support Chomsky's innatist position:

1 Virtually all children successfully learn their native language at a time in life when they would not be expected to learn anything else so complicated.

2 Children successfully master the basic structure of their native language or dialect in a variety of conditions: some which would be expected to enhance language development (for example, caring, attentive parents who focus on the child's language), and some which might be expected to inhibit it (for example, abusive or rejecting parents). Children achieve different levels of vocabulary, creativity, social grace, and so on, but virtually all achieve mastery of the *structure* of the language spoken around them.

3 The language children are exposed to does not contain examples of all the information which they eventually know.

4 Animals—even primates receiving intensive training from humans—cannot learn to manipulate a symbol system as complicated as the natural language of a three- or four-year-old human child.

5 Children seem to accomplish the complex task of language acquisition without having someone consistently point out to them *which* of the sentences they hear and produce are 'correct' and which are 'ungrammatical'.

One example of the kind of complex language systems which children seem to learn without special guidance is the system of reflexive pronouns. This system of pronouns has been studied by a number of linguists working from a Chomskyan perspective. Consider the following sentences which we have taken from a recent book by Lydia White (1989). These English sentences contain the reflexive pronoun 'himself'. Both the pronoun and the noun it refers to (the antecedent) are printed in italics. An asterisk at the beginning of a sentence indicates that the sentence is ungrammatical.

What do children have to discover about the relationship between the reflexive pronoun and its antecedent?

    a. *John* saw *himself.*
    b. **Himself* saw *John.*

In (a) and (b), it looks as if the reflexive pronoun must follow the noun it refers to. But (c) disproves this:

    c. Looking after *himself* bores *John.*

If we consider sentences such as:

    d. John said that *Fred* liked *himself.*
    e. **John* said that Fred liked *himself.*
    f. John told *Bill* to wash *himself.*
    g. **John* told Bill to wash *himself.*

we might conclude that the closest noun phrase is usually the antecedent. However, (h) shows that this rule won't work either:

    h. *John* promised Bill to wash *himself.*

And it's even more complicated than that. Usually the reflexive must be in the same clause as the antecedent as in (a) and (d), but not always, as in (h). Furthermore, the reflexive can be in the subject position in (i) but not in (j).

    i. *John* believes *himself* to be intelligent (non-finite clause).
    j. **John* believes that *himself* is intelligent (finite clause).

In some cases, more than one antecedent is possible, as in (k) where the reflexive could refer to either John or Bill:

    k. *John* showed *Bill* a picture of *himself.*

By now, you are probably quite convinced of the complexity of the rules pertaining to interpreting reflexive pronouns in English. The innatists argue that children could not discover the distribution of reflexive pronouns by trial and error. In fact, they simply do not make enough mistakes for this explanation to be plausible. The innatists conclude that a child's acquisition of these grammatical rules is guided by principles of an innate Universal Grammar. The child comes to 'know' certain things about the language simply by being exposed to a limited number of examples. Different languages have different rules about, for example, reflexives, and the child seems able to learn, on hearing *some* sentences, which *other* ones are possible and which are *not.*

Biological basis for the innatist position

Chomsky's ideas are compatible with those of biologist Eric Lenneberg who also compares learning to talk with learning to walk: children who for medical reasons cannot move about when infants may soon stand and walk if their problems are corrected at the age of a year or so. Similarly, children who can hear but who cannot speak can nevertheless learn language, understanding even complex sentences.

The 'critical period' hypothesis

Lenneberg observed that this ability to develop normal behaviours and knowledge in a variety of environments does not continue indefinitely and that children who have never learned language (because of deafness or extreme isolation) cannot return to normal if these deprivations go on for too long. He argued that the language acquisition device, like other biological functions, works successfully only when it is stimulated at the right time—a time which is referred to as the 'critical period'.

This notion that there is a specific and limited time period for language acquisition is referred to as the *critical period hypothesis* (CPH). There are two versions of the CPH. The strong version is that children must acquire their *first language* by puberty or they will never be able to learn from subsequent exposure. The weak version is that language learning will be more difficult and incomplete after puberty.

Read the following case studies and think about whether they support either the weak or the strong version of the CPH.

Natural experiments: Victor and Genie

It is understandably difficult to find evidence for the critical period hypothesis, since all normal children are exposed to language at an early age and consequently acquire language. However, history has documented a few 'natural experiments' where children have been deprived of contact with language. One of the most famous cases is that of a child called Victor. François Truffaut created a film, *L'Enfant sauvage* (*The Untamed Child*), about him and about the efforts to teach him to speak. In 1799 a 12-year-old boy was found wandering naked in the woods of Aveyron in France. Upon capture, he was found to be completely wild, apparently having had no contact with humankind. A young doctor, Jean-Marc-Gaspard Itard, devoted five years to the task of civilizing Victor and teaching him language.

Although Itard succeeded to some extent in developing Victor's sociability, memory, judgement, and all the functions of his senses, Victor remained unreceptive to all sounds other than those which had meaning for him in the forest, such as the cracking of a nut, animal sounds, or the sound of rain. He only succeeded in speaking two words, his favourite food 'lait' (milk) and his governess's frequent exclamation 'O Dieu!' (Oh, God!). Moreover, his use of 'lait' was only uttered as an excited exclamation at the sight of a glass of milk. He could not be brought to call for the one object he was capable of naming. Even when Itard deprived Victor of milk in hopes of making him call for it, Victor never used the word to communicate his need. Finally, Itard gave up.

Another famous case of a child who did not learn language normally in her early years is that of Genie. Genie was discovered in 1970, a thirteen-and-a-

half-year-old girl who had been almost completely isolated, deprived, neg-
lected, and abused since the age of 20 months. Because of the irrational
demands of a disturbed father and the submission and fear of an abused
mother, Genie had spent more than eleven years tied to a chair or a crib in a
small, darkened room. Her father had forbidden his wife and son to speak to
her and had himself only growled and barked at her. She was beaten every
time she vocalized or made any kind of noise, and she had long since resorted
to complete silence. Genie was unsocialized, primitive, and undeveloped
physically, emotionally, and intellectually. Needless to say, Genie had no
language.

After she was discovered, Genie was cared for and educated in the most natural surroundings possible, and to the fullest extent possible, with the parti-
cipation of many teachers and therapists. After a brief period in a
rehabilitation centre, Genie lived in a normal, loving foster home and
attended special schools. Although far from being 'normal', Genie made
remarkable progress in becoming socialized and cognitively aware. She developed deep personal relationships and strong individual tastes and traits.
But despite the natural environment for language acquisition, Genie's language development has not paralleled natural first language development.
After five years of exposure to language, a period during which a normal
child would have acquired an elaborated language system, Genie's language
contained many of the features of abnormal language development. These
include a larger than normal gap between comprehension and production,
inconsistency in the use of grammatical forms, a slow *rate of development,*
over-use of formulaic and routine speech, and the absence of some specific
syntactic forms and mechanisms always present in normal grammatical development (Curtiss 1977). For discussion of further developments in
Genie's life, see Rymer (1993).

Genie's language shares features of language development exhibited by
adults with brain damage who have had to re-learn language in adulthood,
by children in the earliest stage of language acquisition, and by chimps
attempting to learn language. It is the most carefully documented and tested
case of a child brought up in isolation, allowing linguists to study the
hypotheses regarding the critical period.

Genie's case seems to support a weak version of the critical period hypothesis, while Victor's case seems to support a strong version. However, it is
difficult to support the CPH with examples from such unusual children
because the unknown circumstances of their early lives make it unclear as to
what other factors (for example, social isolation or physical abuse) might be
contributing to their inability to learn language. For now, the best evidence
for the CPH is that virtually every child learns language on a schedule which
is very similar in spite of quite different circumstances of life. We will return

to a discussion of the CPH in Chapter 3 when we look at the age issue in second language acquisition.

Both Victor and Genie were deprived of a normal home environment, which may account for their abnormal language development. There are other individuals, however, who come from loving homes, yet do not receive exposure to language at the usual time. This is the case of many profoundly deaf children who have hearing parents.

Natural experiments: deaf signers

Elissa Newport and her colleagues have studied deaf users of American Sign Language (ASL) who acquired it as their first language at different ages. Such a population exists because only five to ten per cent of the profoundly deaf are born to deaf parents, and only these would be likely to be exposed to ASL from birth. The remainder of the profoundly deaf population begin learning ASL at different ages, usually when they start attending a residential school where sign language is used for day-to-day communication.

In one study, there were three distinct groups of ASL users: Native signers who were exposed to sign language from birth, Early learners whose first exposure to ASL began at age four to six at school, and Late learners who first came into contact with ASL after the age of twelve (Newport 1990).

The researchers were interested in whether there is any difference between Native signers, Early learners, and Late learners in the ability to produce and comprehend grammatical structures. Just like oral languages, ASL makes use of grammatical markers (like *-ed* and *-ing* in English); the only difference is that these markers are indicated through specific hand movements.

Results of the research showed a clear pattern. On word order, there was no difference between the groups. But on tests focusing on grammatical markers, the Native group outperformed the Early learner group who outperformed the Late learner group. The Native signers were highly consistent in their use of the grammatical forms. Although the other two groups used many of the same forms as the Native group, they also used forms which are considered ungrammatical by the Native signers. For example, they would omit certain grammatical forms, or use them in some *obligatory contexts* but not in others. The researchers conclude that their study supports the hypothesis that there is a critical period for first language acquisition.

Mom's the word: the interactionist position

A third theoretical position focuses on the role of the linguistic environment in interaction with the child's innate capacities in determining language development.

The *interactionists'* position is that language develops as a result of the complex interplay between the uniquely human characteristics of the child and the environment in which the child develops. Unlike the innatists, the interactionists claim that language which is modified to suit the capability of the learner is a *crucial* element in the language acquisition process.

Caretaker talk

Many researchers from the interactionist perspective have studied the speech directed to children. This distinct speech is known as 'motherese' or *caretaker talk*. We are all familiar with the way adults typically modify the way they speak when addressing little children. In English, caretaker talk involves a slower rate of speech, higher pitch, more varied intonation, shorter, simpler sentence patterns, frequent repetition, and paraphrase. Furthermore, topics of conversation are often limited to the child's immediate environment, the 'here and now'. Adults often repeat the content of a child's utterance, but they do so with a grammatically correct sentence.

If you examine the transcripts presented earlier in this chapter, you'll see examples of some of these features. For example, when Peter says, 'Dump truck! Dump truck! Fall! Fall!', Lois responds, 'Yes, the dump truck fell down.'

It is difficult to judge the importance of these modifications which adults make in speech addressed to children. The evidence suggests that children whose parents do not consistently provide such *modified interaction* will still learn language, but these children may have access to the modified speech when they are in the company of older siblings or other adults. To the interactionists, what is important is the conversational give-and-take in which the adult intuitively responds to the clues the child provides as to the level of language he or she is capable of processing. The importance of child-adult interaction becomes abundantly clear in the atypical cases where it is missing such as that of Jim.

Case study: Jim

Jim, the hearing child of deaf parents, had little contact with hearing adults up to the age of three years and nine months (3,9). His only contact with oral language was through television which he watched frequently. The family was unusual in that the parents did not use sign language with Jim. Although in other respects he was well cared for, Jim did not begin his linguistic development in a normal environment in which a parent communicated with him in either oral or sign language.

Language tests administered when Jim was 3,9 indicated that he was very much below age level in all aspects of language. Although he attempted to express ideas appropriate to his age, he used unusual, ungrammatical word order.

When Jim began conversational sessions with an adult, his expressive abilities began to improve. By the age of 4,2 most of the unusual speech patterns had disappeared, replaced by structures typical for Jim's age. It is interesting to note that Jim's younger brother Glenn did not display the same type of lag and performed normally on language tests when he was the age at which Jim was first tested. It should be noted that his linguistic environment was different in that he had his older brother as a conversational partner (Sachs, Bard, and Johnson 1981).

Jim showed dramatic acquisition of the structures of English once he began to interact with an adult on a one-to-one basis. The fact that he had failed to acquire language normally prior to that suggests that the problem lay in the environment, not the child. That is, it seems that exposure to impersonal sources of language (such as television or radio) alone is insufficient for the child to learn the structure of a particular language.

One-to-one interaction gives the child access to language which is adjusted to his or her level of comprehension. When a child does not understand, the adult may repeat or paraphrase. The response of the adult may also allow children to find out when their own utterances are understood. Television, for obvious reasons, does not provide such interaction. Even in children's programs, where simpler language is used and topics are relevant to younger viewers, there is no immediate adjustment made for the needs of an individual child.

Summary

We have presented three different theories of language acquisition, each of which can be corroborated by evidence. As we have seen in the transcripts from Peter and Cindy (pages 3 and 4), children *do* imitate and practise, and that practice can explain how some aspects of the language such as word meanings and some language routines are learned. We saw in the example of reflexive pronouns, however, that imitation and practice alone cannot account for the complexity of the knowledge that all children eventually attain. The acquisition of such complex language seems to depend on children's possession of some knowledge which permits them to process the language they hear and to go well beyond these and even beyond simple generalizations. The discussion of the interactionist position (especially the case of Jim) showed that children who are exposed to language in the absence of one-to-one interaction do not develop language normally.

One way to reconcile the behaviourist, innatist, and interactionist explanations is to see that each may help to explain a different aspect of children's language development. Behaviourist explanations may explain routine aspects, while innatist explanations seem most plausible in explaining the acquisition of complex grammar. Interactionist explanations are necessary for understanding how children relate form and meaning in language, how they interact in conversations, and how they use language appropriately.

In Chapter 2 we will begin to look at the acquisition of second languages by children and older learners. We will see that many of the issues raised in this chapter will be relevant to our discussion of second language acquisition as well.

Sources and suggestions for further reading

General accounts of first language acquisition

Baron, N. 1992. *Growing Up with Language*. Reading, Mass.: Addison-Wesley.

Bloom, L. and **M. Lahey.** 1978. *Language Development and Language Disorders*. New York: John Wiley and Sons.

de Villiers, J. G. and **P. A. de Villiers.** 1978. *Language Acquisition*. Cambridge, Mass.: Harvard University Press.

Ingram, D. 1989. *First Language Acquisition: Method, Description and Explanation*. Cambridge: Cambridge University Press.

Chomsky's innatist ideas

Chomsky, N. 1959. Review of *Verbal Behavior* by B.F. Skinner. *Language* 35: 26–58.

Chomsky, N. 1981. *Lectures on Government and Binding.* Dordrecht: Foris. Chapter 1.

Cook, V. 1988. *Chomsky's Universal Grammar.* London: Basil Blackwell.

White, L. 1989. *Universal Grammar and Second Language Acquisition.* Amsterdam/Philadelphia, Pa.: John Benjamins.

Genie

Curtiss, S. 1977. *Genie: A Psycholinguistic Study of a Modern-day 'Wild Child.'* New York: Academic Press.

Rymer, R. 1993. *Genie: An Abused Child's Flight from Silence.* London: Michael Joseph.

L'enfant sauvage

Itard, J.-M.-G. 1962. *The Wild Boy of Aveyron (L'Enfant sauvage).* New York: Meredith.

Learning American Sign Language at different ages

Newport, E. 1990. 'Maturational constraints on language learning.' *Cognitive Science* 14: 11–28.

Case study of Jim

Sachs, J., B. Bard, and M. Johnson. 1981. 'Language learning with restricted input: Case studies of two hearing children of deaf parents.' *Applied Psycholinguistics* 2: 33–54.

2 THEORIES OF SECOND LANGUAGE LEARNING

In this chapter we look at some of the theories that have been proposed to account for *second language acquisition* (SLA). In many ways, theories which have been developed for SLA are closely related to those discussed for first language acquisition in Chapter 1. That is, some theories give primary importance to the learners' innate characteristics; some emphasize the essential role of environment in shaping language learning; still others seek to integrate learner characteristics and environmental factors in their explanation for how second language acquisition takes place.

It is clear, however, that a child or adult acquiring a second language is different from a child acquiring a first language in terms of both personal characteristics and conditions for learning. In addition, any given second language learner may differ from another second language learner in many ways. Consider, for example, the following second language learner profiles: a pre-school child learning a second language from playmates in a bilingual setting, an adolescent student learning a second language formally in a foreign language classroom, and an adult immigrant learning the second language in an *informal language learning setting*, at work and in daily life. Is age the only difference? How are the conditions for language learning different? For example:

1 Does the learner already know a language?

2 Is the learner cognitively mature, that is, is he or she able to engage in problem solving, deduction, and complex memory tasks?

3 How well developed is the learner's *metalinguistic awareness*? That is, can the learner treat language as an object—for example, define a word, say what sounds make up that word, or state a rule such as 'add an -s to form the plural'?

4 How extensive is the learner's general knowledge of the world? This kind of knowledge makes it easier to understand language because one can sometimes make good guesses about what the interlocutor is probably saying even when the language carrying the message is very difficult.

5 Is the learner nervous about making mistakes and sounding 'silly' when speaking the language?

6 Does the learning environment allow the learner to be silent in the early stages of learning, or is he or she expected to speak from the beginning?

7 Is there plenty of time available for language learning to take place, plenty of contact with proficient speakers of the language?

8 Does the learner receive *corrective feedback* when he or she makes errors in grammar or pronunciation, or does the listener overlook these errors and pay attention to the message?

9 Does the learner receive corrective feedback when he or she uses the wrong word, or does the listener usually try to guess the intended meaning?

10 Is the learner exposed to language which is at an appropriate level of difficulty in terms of speed of delivery, complexity of grammatical structure, and vocabulary?

Activity

Learner profiles

The chart in Table 2.1 helps to illustrate possible answers to these questions with respect to the profiles of four language learners: a child learning its first language; a child learning a second language informally; an adolescent learning a second language in a *formal language learning setting*; an adult learning the language informally (in the workplace or among friends). Fill in the chart, giving your opinion about the presence or absence of the characteristics or conditions referred to in the questions above. Use the following notation: '+' for a characteristic which is usually present, '–' when it is usually absent, and '?' for cases where the characteristic or condition is sometimes present, sometimes absent, or where you are not sure of your opinion.

Table 2.1: Profiles of language learners: learner characteristics and learning conditions

			L2	
Learner characteristics	*Child L1*	*Child (informal)*	*Adolescent (formal)*	*Adult (informal)*
1 knowledge of another language				
2 cognitive maturity				
3 metalinguistic awareness				
4 knowledge of the world				
5 nervousness about speaking				
Learning conditions				
6 freedom to be silent				
7 ample time				
8 corrective feedback: grammar and pronunciation				
9 corrective feedback: word choice				
10 modified input				

The discussion below summarizes our views about the profiles of these four language learners in terms of their characteristics and the conditions in which their learning takes place.

Learner characteristics

All second language learners, regardless of age, have *by definition* already acquired at least one language. This prior knowledge may be an advantage in the sense that the learner has an idea of how languages work. On the other hand, as we shall see, knowledge of other languages can also lead learners to make incorrect guesses about how the second language works and this may cause errors which a learner of a first language would not make.

Young second language learners begin the task of language learning without the benefit of some of the skills and knowledge which adolescent and adult learners have. The first language learner does not have the *cognitive maturity*, metalinguistic awareness, or world knowledge of the older second language learner. Nor, on the other hand, do most young learners feel nervous about attempting to use the language—even when their proficiency is quite limited.

Depending on their age, young second language learners have begun to develop cognitive maturity and metalinguistic awareness. They will still have far to go in these areas, as well as in the area of world knowledge, before they reach the levels already attained by adults and adolescents. Even very young (pre-school) children differ in their nervousness when faced with speaking a language they do not know well. Some children happily chatter away in their new language; others prefer to listen and participate silently in social interaction with their peers. Fortunately for these children, the learning environment rarely puts pressure on them to speak when they are not ready.

Learning conditions

No adolescent or adult has the same experiences as young children enjoy. Younger learners in an informal second language learning environment are allowed to be silent until they are ready to speak, while older learners are often forced to speak—to meet the requirements of a classroom or to carry out everyday tasks such as shopping, medical visits, or job interviews. Young children in informal settings are usually exposed to the second language for many hours every day. Older learners, especially students in language classrooms, are more likely to receive only limited exposure to the second language.

One condition which appears to be common to learners of all ages is access to *modified input*. This adjusted speech style is called *caretaker talk* for first languages, and *foreigner talk* or *teacher talk* for second languages. Most people who interact regularly with language learners seem to have an intuitive sense of what adjustments are needed to help learners understand. Of course, some people are better at this than others. We have all witnessed those painful conversations in which insensitive people seem to think that they can make learners understand better if they simply talk louder!

Error correction, as noted in Chapter 1, tends to be limited to corrections of meaning—including errors in vocabulary choice—in first language acquisition. In informal second language acquisition, errors which do not interfere with meaning are usually overlooked. Most people would feel they were being impolite if they interrupted and corrected someone who was trying to have a conversation with them! Nevertheless, they may 'correct' if they cannot understand what the speaker is trying to say. Thus, errors of grammar and pronunciation are rarely remarked on, but the wrong word choice may receive comment from a puzzled interlocutor. The only place where error correction is typically present with high frequency is the language classroom.

Summary
The completed chart in Table 2.1 shows that second language learners of different ages have different characteristics and access to different conditions for learning. A general theory of SLA will need to account for language acquisition by learners with a variety of characteristics, learning in a variety of different contexts. We now turn to four theoretical perspectives which seek to do that.

Behaviourism: the second language view

According to the behaviourists, all learning, whether verbal or non-verbal, takes place through the same underlying process, habit formation. Learners receive linguistic *input* from speakers in their environment, and positive re-inforcement for their correct repetitions and imitations. As a result, habits are formed. Because language development is described as the acquisition of a set of habits, it is assumed that a person learning a second language starts off with the habits associated with the first language. These habits interfere with those needed for second language speech, and new habits must be formed (Lado 1964).

For the behaviourist, errors are seen as first language habits interfering with the acquisition of second language habits. This psychological learning theory has often been linked to the *contrastive analysis hypothesis* (CAH). The CAH predicts that where there are similarities between the two languages, the learner will acquire *target language* structures with ease; where there are differences, the learner will have difficulty. As we shall see, there is little doubt that a learner's first language influences the acquisition of a second language. However, it is not the case that the influence is simply a matter of 'habits', but rather a systematic attempt by the learner to use knowledge already acquired in learning a new language.

Researchers have found that not all errors predicted by the CAH are actually made. Furthermore, learners do make many errors which are not predictable on the basis of the CAH. For example, adult beginners use simple structures in the target language just as children do: 'No understand' or 'Yesterday I meet my teacher'. What is more, the features of these simple structures are very similar across learners from a variety of backgrounds, even if the structures of their respective first languages are different from each other and different from English.

A traditional version of the CAH would predict that where differences exist, errors would be bi-directional, that is, for example, French speakers learning English and English speakers learning French would make errors on parallel linguistic features. To illustrate this, let us examine one way in which French and English differ and how this might be expected to lead to errors.

In English, direct objects, whether nouns or pronouns, come after the verb (for example, 'The dog eats *it*, the dog eats *the cookie*'). In French, direct objects which are nouns follow the verb (for example, 'Le chien mange *le biscuit*'—literally, 'The dog eats the biscuit'), but pronoun direct objects precede the verb (for example, 'Le chien *le* mange'—literally, 'The dog it eats'). The CAH would predict that a *native speaker* of English might say: 'Le chien mange *le*' when speaking French, and that a native speaker of French might say 'The dog *it* ate' when speaking English.

In fact, research has shown that English speakers learning French are more likely to make the predicted error than French speakers learning English. This may be due to the fact that English speakers learning French hear many examples of sentences with subject-verb-object word order in French (for example, 'Le chien mange le biscuit'). Thus they make the incorrect assumption—based on both the word order of their first language *and* information from their second language—that pronoun objects, like noun objects, come after the verb. French-speaking learners of English, on the other hand, hearing and seeing no evidence that English pronoun objects precede verbs, make this error very rarely indeed. Researchers have also found that learners have intuitions that certain features of their first language are less likely to be *transferable* than others. For example, most learners know intuitively that idiomatic or metaphorical expressions cannot simply be translated word for word.

All this suggests that the influence of the learner's first language is not simply a matter of habits, but a much more subtle and complex process of identifying points of similarity, weighing the evidence in support of some particular feature, and even reflecting (though not necessarily consciously) about whether a certain feature seems to 'belong' in the structure of the target language.

As in first language acquisition, the behaviourist account has proven to be at best an incomplete explanation of second language acquisition. Psychologists and language acquisitions researchers have moved on to new, more complex theories of learning.

Cognitive theory: a new psychological approach

Cognitive psychologists tend to see second language acquisition as the building up of knowledge systems that can eventually be called on automatically for speaking and understanding. At first, learners have to pay attention to any aspect of the language which they are trying to understand or produce. Gradually, through experience and practice, learners become able to use certain parts of their knowledge so quickly and automatically that they are not even aware that they are doing it. This frees them to focus on other aspects of the language which, in turn, gradually become automatic (McLaughlin 1987).

Recently, cognitive psychologists have also investigated a phenomenon they call 'restructuring'. This refers to the observation that sometimes things which we know and use automatically may not be explainable in terms of a gradual build-up of automaticity through practice. They seem rather to be based on the interaction of knowledge we already have, or on the acquisition of new knowledge which—without extensive practice—somehow 'fits' into an existing system and may, in fact, 'restructure' this system. This may lead to sudden bursts of progress for the learner, but it can also sometimes lead to apparent back-sliding when a systematic aspect of learner language suddenly incorporates too much or incorporates the wrong things.

Cognitive theory is a relative newcomer to SLA research, and has not yet been widely tested empirically. Because the theory itself cannot easily predict what kinds of structures will be automatized through practice and what will be restructured, direct applications of this theory for classroom teaching are premature. Cognitive theory is also not able to predict which first language structures will be transferred and which will not. This theory, which looks at the learning process, is incomplete without a linguistic framework of some kind. This has led some cognitive psychologists to seek collaboration with linguists so that the aspects of language which are studied will have clearer relevance to the complex phenomenon of second language acquisition.

Creative construction theory

Although Chomsky does not himself discuss the implications of his innatist theory for second language learning, others have proposed a position which is, in some respects, similar to Chomsky's ideas on first language learning. This theory is sometimes called the *creative construction* hypothesis. Learners are thought to 'construct' internal representations of the language being learned. One may think of these internal representations as 'mental pictures' of the target language. The internal representations are thought to develop, in predictable stages, in the direction of the full second language system.

Most of the evidence for this theory has come from the analysis of learners' errors at various points in their second language acquisition, and the order or sequence in which certain structures are acquired. What is distinctive about this theory is that it proposes that internal processing strategies operate on language input without any direct dependence on the learner actually producing the language. That is, the learner need not actually speak or write in order to acquire language. Acquisition takes place internally as learners read and hear samples of the language that they understand. The speech and writing which the learner eventually produces is seen as an outcome of the learning process rather than as the cause of learning or even as a necessary step in learning. Learners' oral or written production is useful only in so far as it allows the learner to participate in communicative situations. The creative construction theory which has had the most influence on second language teaching practice is the one proposed by Stephen Krashen (1982).

In a series of papers and books, Krashen has developed an overall theory of second language acquisition which attempts to bring together research findings from a number of diverse areas. Five central hypotheses constitute his 'monitor model', and Krashen claims that research findings from a number of different domains are consistent with these five basic hypotheses. They are: (1) the acquisition-learning hypothesis; (2) the monitor hypothesis; (3) the natural order hypothesis; (4) the input hypothesis; and (5) the affective filter hypothesis.

1 The acquisition-learning hypothesis

According to Krashen, there are two ways for adult second language learners to approach learning a second language: they may 'acquire' it or they may 'learn' it. Essentially, he says, we acquire as we engage in meaningful interaction in the second language, in much the same way that children pick up their first language—with no attention to form. We learn, on the other hand, via a conscious process of study and attention to form and error correction, most typically in formal language classrooms.

For Krashen, acquisition is by far the more important process. He asserts that it is only acquired language which is readily available for natural, fluent communication. Further, he asserts that learning cannot turn into acquisition, citing as evidence for this that many speakers are quite competent without ever having learned rules, while other speakers may 'know' rules but continue to break them when they are focusing their attention on meaningful interaction rather than on the application of grammatical rules for accurate performance.

Unfortunately, it would be extremely difficult to detect which system, acquisition or learning, is at work at any given moment. To test this hypothesis, each of these abstractions (acquisition and learning) would need to be defined more sharply, and controlled and manipulated experimentally, and this has proved very difficult to do.

2 The monitor hypothesis

Krashen argues that the acquired system acts to initiate the speaker's utterances and is responsible for fluency and intuitive judgements about correctness. The learned system, on the other hand, acts only as an editor or 'monitor', making minor changes and polishing what the acquired system has produced. Moreover, Krashen has specified three conditions necessary for monitor use: sufficient time, focus on form, and knowing the rules. Thus, writing is more conducive to monitor use than is speaking, where the focus is on content and not on form. He maintains that knowing the rules only helps the speaker polish what has been acquired via real communication, and that the focus of language teaching should therefore be communication and not rule-learning.

The obvious weakness in this hypothesis is that it is very difficult to show evidence of 'monitor' use. In any given utterance, it is impossible to determine what has been produced by the acquired system and what is the result of monitor use. Krashen's claim that 'learning cannot turn into acquisition' means that anything which is produced quickly and apparently spontaneously must have been acquired rather than learned. This leaves us with a somewhat circular definition, one which is difficult to explore with research.

3 The natural order hypothesis

This hypothesis states that we acquire the rules of a language in a predictable sequence—some rules are acquired early while others are acquired late.

Contrary to intuition, the rules which are easiest to state (and thus easy to 'learn') are not necessarily the first to be acquired (for example, the rule for adding an -*s* to third person singular verbs in the present tense). Further, Krashen asserts that the *natural order* is independent of the order in which rules have been taught. Most of the evidence for this hypothesis comes from the *morpheme* studies, in which children's speech has been examined for accuracy of certain *grammatical morphemes* (mostly noun and verb 'endings' such as plural -*s* and past tense -*ed* in English). A large number of studies have provided evidence that learners pass through similar sequences or stages in development. In Chapter 4, we will look at some of these acquisition sequences in second language acquisition, including the 'morpheme' studies.

4 *The input hypothesis*

Krashen asserts that we acquire language in only one way – by receiving *comprehensible input*, that is, by understanding messages. If the input contains forms and structures just beyond the learner's current level of competence in the language, then both comprehension and acquisition will occur.

Krashen cites many varied lines of evidence for this hypothesis, most of which appeal to intuition, but which have never been substantiated by empirical studies. In his later writings, Krashen admits that comprehensible input is a necessary but not a sufficient condition for acquisition. The other necessary condition relates to hypothesis 5.

5 *The affective filter hypothesis*

The 'affective filter' is an imaginary barrier which prevents learners from using input which is available in the environment. 'Affect' refers to such things as motives, needs, attitudes, and emotional states. A learner who is tense, angry, anxious, or bored will screen out input, making it unavailable for acquisition. Thus, depending on the learner's state of mind or disposition, the filter limits what is attended to and what is acquired. The filter will be 'up' or operating when the learner is stressed, self-conscious, or unmotivated. It will be 'down' when the learner is relaxed and motivated.

What makes this hypothesis attractive to practitioners is that it appears to have immediate implications for classroom practice. Teachers can understand why some learners, given the same opportunity to learn, may be successful while others are not. It also appeals intuitively to those who have tried unsuccessfully to learn a language in conditions where they felt stressed or uncomfortable. The difficulty with the hypothesis is that, like the research related to the role of motivation (discussed in Chapter 3), it is difficult to be sure that the affective factors *cause* the differences in language acquisition. It

seems likely that success in acquisition may in itself contribute to more positive motivation or, in Krashen's terms, to a 'lowered affective filter'.

Summary

Krashen's writing has been very influential in strengthening the recent focus on *communicative language teaching*, particularly in North America. On the other hand, the theory has also been seriously criticized for failing to meet certain minimum standards necessary in scientific research and writing. Most teachers and researchers see in the creative construction theories much which is intuitively appealing. There is, however, a great deal of research required before the details spelled out in, for example, Krashen's Monitor Model can be taken as adequately supported.

The second language interactionist view

As indicated in Chapter 1, interactionists claim that a crucial element in the language acquisition process is the modified input that learners are exposed to and the way in which native speakers interact in conversations with learners.

Proponents of the interactionist view such as Michael Long agree with Krashen that comprehensible input is necessary for language acquisition. However, they are more concerned with the question of *how* input is made comprehensible. They see interactional modifications which take place in conversations between native speakers and non-native speakers as the necessary mechanism for this to take place (Long 1985).

For Long and others, *modified interaction* must be necessary for language acquisition. This relationship has been summarized as follows:

1 Interactional modification makes input comprehensible;

2 Comprehensible input promotes acquisition.

Therefore,

3 Interactional modification promotes acquisition.

Long argues that there are no cases of beginning-level learners acquiring a second language from native-speaker talk which has *not* been modified in some way. In fact, research shows that native speakers consistently modify their speech in sustained conversation with non-native speakers. Some examples of these conversational modifications are:

1 Comprehension checks—efforts by the native speaker to determine that the learner understands (for example, 'The bus leaves at 6:30. Do you understand?')

2 Clarification requests—efforts to get the learner to clarify something which has not been understood (for example, 'Could you say that again?')

3 Self-repetition or paraphrase—the native speaker repeats his or her sentence either partially or in its entirety. (For example, 'She got lost on her way home from school. She was walking home from school. She got lost.')

Research which has been carried out to investigate these relationships has demonstrated that conversational adjustments can aid comprehension. However, no research has provided direct evidence for the second claim, which is more difficult to measure—that comprehensible input causes or explains acquisition.

Summary

Although other theories of SLA have been proposed in the literature, we have chosen to focus our discussion on only four of them here. Moreover, the SLA theories presented in this chapter represent views which are based on the assumption that first language and second language learning are similar. There are other SLA theories, however, which point to key differences between first language and second language learning. For example, some theorists insist that creative construction and interactionist theories, while they may be able to explain some aspects of the development of fluency and interactive confidence, are not satisfactory for explaining how second language learners eventually master the grammatical or phonological systems of the target language. They argue that older learners, especially adults, will not reach their highest potential in SLA without some explicit guidance in identifying differences between their own use of the target language and that of proficient speakers. This will be discussed in Chapter 5 when we examine some of the research on learning second languages in an instructional environment.

Sources and suggestions for further reading

General discussion of theories of second language acquisition

Cook, V. 1991. *Second Language Learning and Language Teaching.* London: Edward Arnold.

Ellis, R. 1986. *Understanding Second Language Acquisition.* Oxford: Oxford University Press.

Ellis, R. 1994. *The Study of Second Language Acquisition.* Oxford: Oxford University Press.

Larsen-Freeman, D., and **M. H. Long.** 1991. *An Introduction to Second Language Acquisition Research.* New York: Longman.

Lightbown, P. M. 1985. 'Great expectations: Second language acquisition research and classroom teaching.' *Applied Linguistics* 6/2: 173–89.

Behaviourism in SLA

Lado, R. 1964. *Language Teaching: A Scientific Approach.* New York: McGraw-Hill.

Cognitive theory

McLaughlin, B. 1987. *Theories of Second Language Learning.* London: Edward Arnold.

Creative construction

Dulay, H., M. Burt, and **S. Krashen.** 1982. *Language Two.* Oxford: Oxford University Press.

Krashen, S. 1982. *Principles and Practice in Second Language Acquisition.* Oxford: Pergamon.

Interactionism in SLA

Long, M. H. 1985. 'Input and second language acquisition theory' in S. Gass and C. Madden (eds.): *Input in Second Language Acquisition* . Rowley, Mass.: Newbury House (pp. 377–93).

3 FACTORS AFFECTING SECOND LANGUAGE LEARNING

In Chapter 1, it was pointed out that all normal children, given a normal up-bringing, are successful in the acquisition of their first language. This contrasts with our experience of second language learners, who vary greatly in their abilities to acquire their second language.

Many of us believe that learners have certain characteristics which lead to more or less successful language learning. Such beliefs are usually based on anecdotal evidence, that is, on individual people we have known. For example, many teachers are convinced that extroverted learners who interact without inhibition in their second language and find many opportunities to practise language skills will be the most successful learners. In addition to personality characteristics, other factors generally considered to be relevant to language learning are intelligence, aptitude, motivation, and attitudes. Another important factor, as our previous discussion of the critical period hypothesis for first language acquisition has suggested, is the age at which learning begins.

In this chapter, we will see whether anecdotal evidence is supported by research findings. To what extent can we predict differences in the success of second language acquisition in two individuals if we have information about their personalities, their general and specific intellectual abilities, their motivation, or their age?

Activity

Characteristics of the 'good language learner'

It seems that some people have a much easier time of learning languages than others. Rate of development varies widely among first language learners. Some children can string together five-, six-, and seven-word sentences at the same time that other children are just beginning to label items in their immediate environment. Nevertheless, all normal children eventually master their first language.

In second language learning, it has been observed countless times that in the same classroom setting, some students progress rapidly through the initial stages of a new language while others struggle along making very slow progress. Some learners never achieve *native-like* command of a second language. Are there personal characteristics that make one learner more successful than the other, and if so, what are they?

The following is a list of some of the characteristics commonly thought to contribute to successful language learning. In your experience—as a second language learner and as a teacher—which characteristics seem to you most likely to be associated with success in second language acquisition in the classroom? Which ones would you be less inclined to expect in a successful learner?

In each case rate the characteristic as follows:

1 = Very important
2 = Quite important
3 = Important
4 = Not very important
5 = Not at all important.

A good language learner:

a	is a willing and accurate guesser	I	2	3	4	5
b	tries to get a message across even if specific language knowledge is lacking	I	2	3	4	5
c	is willing to make mistakes	I	2	3	4	5
d	constantly looks for patterns in the language	I	2	3	4	5
e	practises as often as possible	I	2	3	4	5
f	analyses his or her own speech and the speech of others	I	2	3	4	5
g	attends to whether his or her performance meets the standards he or she has learned	I	2	3	4	5
h	enjoys grammar exercises	I	2	3	4	5
i	begins learning in childhood	I	2	3	4	5
j	has an above-average IQ	I	2	3	4	5
k	has good academic skills	I	2	3	4	5
l	has a good self-image and lots of confidence	I	2	3	4	5

All of the characteristics listed above can be classified into five main categories: motivation, aptitude, personality, intelligence, and learning style. However, many of the characteristics cannot be assigned exclusively to one category. For example, the characteristic 'is willing to make mistakes' can be considered a personality and/or a motivational factor if the learner is willing to make mistakes in order to get the message across.

Research on learner characteristics

Perhaps the best way to begin our discussion is to describe how research on the influence of learner characteristics on second language learning has been carried out. When researchers are interested in finding out whether an individual factor such as motivation affects second language learning, they usually select a group of learners and give them a questionnaire to measure the type and degree of motivation. The learners are then given a test to measure their second language proficiency. The test and the questionnaire are both scored and the researcher investigates whether a learner with a high score on the proficiency test is also more likely to have a high score on the motivation questionnaire. If this is the case, the researcher usually concludes that high levels of motivation are correlated with success in language learning. A similar procedure can be used to measure the effects of intelligence on second language learning through the use of IQ tests.

Although this procedure seems straightforward, there are several difficulties with it. The first problem is that it is not possible to directly observe and measure qualities such as aptitude, motivation, extroversion, or even intelligence. These are just labels for an entire range of behaviours and characteristics. Furthermore, because characteristics such as these are not independent, it will come as no surprise that different researchers have often used the same labels to describe different sets of behavioural traits.

For example, in motivation questionnaires, learners are often asked whether they willingly seek out opportunities to use their second language with native speakers and if so, how often they do this. The assumption behind such a question is that learners who report that they often seek out opportunities to interact with speakers of the second language are highly motivated to learn. Although this assumption seems reasonable, it is problematic because if a learner responds by saying 'yes' to this question, it not only suggests that the learner is highly motivated, but also that the learner has more opportunities for language practice in informal contexts. Because it is usually impossible to separate these two factors (i.e. willingness to interact and opportunities to interact), many researchers have been seriously criticized for attempting to present these characteristics as independent.

Another factor which makes it difficult to reach conclusions about relationships between individual learner characteristics and second language learning is how language proficiency is defined and measured. To illustrate this
point let us refer once again to the personal characteristic of motivation. In
the second language learning literature, it is not uncommon to find that
while some studies report that learners with a higher level of motivation are
more successful language learners than those with lower motivation, other
studies report that highly motivated learners do not perform any better on a
proficiency test than learners with much less motivation to learn the second
language. One explanation which has been offered for these conflicting
findings is that the language proficiency tests used in these studies do not
measure the same kind of knowledge. That is, highly motivated learners are
found to be more successful in some studies because the proficiency tests
measure oral communication skills. In other studies, however, highly motivated learners are not found to be more successful because the tests are
primarily measures of grammatical knowledge. Results such as these imply
that motivation to learn a second language may be more related to particular
aspects of language proficiency than to others.

Finally, there is the problem of interpreting the *correlation* of two factors as
being due to a causal relationship between them. That is, the fact that two
things tend to occur together does not necessarily mean that one caused the
other. Research on motivation is perhaps the best context in which to illustrate this. Learners who are successful may indeed be highly motivated. But
can we conclude that they became successful because of their motivation? Is
it not also plausible that their success heightened their motivation? In fact, it
is very difficult to show with certainty that the correlations that are found
between learner characteristics and success in second language acquisition
are indicative of a one-way causal relationship. It seems more likely that, at
least for some of these individual differences, the characteristic may contribute to success, but success also contributes to the enhancement of characteristics such as motivation, risk-taking behaviour, or even performance on
tests which measure aptitude for language learning.

As we will see, research on individual differences often permits multiple
interpretations. In the sections below, we will look at 'what people say'
about individual differences and 'what the research shows' to support or
refute these opinions.

Intelligence

A link between intelligence and second language learning has been reported
by several researchers. Over the years, many studies using a variety of IQ
tests and different methods of assessing language learning have found that
intelligence levels were a good means of predicting how successful a learner

would be at language learning. Furthermore, some recent studies have shown that intelligence may be more strongly related to certain kinds of second language abilities than others. For example, in a study with French *immersion* children in Canada, it was found that while intelligence was related to the development of French second language reading, grammar, and vocabulary, it was unrelated to oral productive skills (Genesee 1976).

Similar findings have been reported in other studies where intelligence was highly related to performance on reading, dictation, and writing tasks, but not on listening comprehension and free oral production tasks. These findings suggest that intelligence is more related to those second language skills which are used in the formal study of a language (i.e. reading, language analysis, writing, and vocabulary study), but that intelligence is much less likely to influence the way in which oral communication skills are developed. Therefore, intelligence seems to be a strong factor when it comes to learning second languages in classrooms, particularly if the instruction is formal. When the classroom instruction is less formal, however (i.e. more communicative), so-called 'intelligence' (as measured by IQ tests) may play a less important role.

Aptitude

There is evidence in the research literature that some individuals have an exceptional 'aptitude' for language learning. Lorraine Obler (1989) reports that a man, whom she calls CJ, has such a specialized ability. CJ is a native speaker of English who grew up in an English home. His first true experience with a second language came at the age of 15 with formal instruction in French. CJ also studied German, Spanish, and Latin while in high school. At age 20, he made a brief visit to Germany. CJ reported that just hearing German spoken for a short time was enough for him to 'recover' the German he had learned in school. Later, CJ worked in Morocco where he reported learning Moroccan Arabic through both formal instruction and informal immersion. He also spent some time in Spain and Italy, where he apparently 'picked up' both Spanish and Italian in a 'matter of weeks'. A remarkable talent indeed!

There may be few learners like CJ, but research does show that human beings exhibit a wide range of aptitude for learning a second language.

The 'aptitude' factor has been investigated most intensively by researchers who are interested in developing tests which can predict how successful a language learner will be. The most widely used aptitude tests are the Modern Language Aptitude Test (MLAT) and the Pimsleur Language Aptitude Battery. Both tests measure characteristics such as: (1) the ability to identify and memorize new sounds; (2) the ability to understand how words function grammatically in sentences; (3) the ability to figure out grammatical rules from language samples; and (4) memory for new words. It is thought that learners will be more successful if they have these abilities.

Although there have been a number of studies examining this factor, the results are in no way conclusive. One of the most serious problems is that it is not clear what the abilities are that constitute aptitude. That is, many of the behaviours associated with it may just as easily be associated with another learner characteristic such as general intelligence or personality. Furthermore, the abilities which are associated with success in an academic course may not be as closely linked to the success some people have in 'picking up' a language.

Personality

A number of personality characteristics have been proposed as likely to affect second language learning, but it has not been easy to demonstrate their effects in empirical studies. As with other research investigating the effects of individual characteristics on second language learning, different studies measuring a similar personality trait produce different results. For example, it is often argued that an extroverted person is well-suited to language learning. However, research does not always support this conclusion. Although some studies have found that success in language learning is highly related to learners' scores on some characteristics often associated with extroversion such as assertiveness and adventurousness, others have found that successful language learners do not get high scores on measures of extroversion.

Another aspect of personality which has been studied is inhibition. It has been suggested that inhibition discourages risk-taking which is necessary for progress in language learning. This is often considered to be a particular problem for adolescents, who are more self-conscious than younger learners. In a series of studies, Alexander Guiora and his colleagues have found support for the claim that inhibition is a negative force in language learning. One study involved an analysis of the effects of small doses of alcohol on pronunciation (Guiora et al. 1972). It was found that *subjects* who received small doses of alcohol did better on pronunciation tests than those who did not drink any alcohol. While results such as these are interesting, as well as amusing, they are not convincing, since experiments such as these are far removed from the reality of the classroom situation. We may also note, in passing, that when larger doses of alcohol were administered, pronunciation rapidly deteriorated!

Several other personality characteristics such as self-esteem, empathy, dominance, talkativeness, and responsiveness, have also been studied. However, in general, the available research does not show a clearly defined relationship between personality and second language acquisition. And, as indicated earlier, the major difficulty in investigating personality characteristics is that of identification and measurement. Another explanation which has been offered for the mixed findings of personality studies is that personality variables may be a major factor only in the acquisition of *communicative competence*. The confused picture of the research on personality factors is due in part to the fact that comparisons are made between studies that measure communicative ability and studies that measure grammatical accuracy or knowledge of linguistic rules. Personality variables seem to be consistently related to the former, but not to the latter.

Despite the inconclusive results and the problems involved in carrying out research in the area of personality characteristics, many researchers believe that personality will be shown to have an important influence on success in language learning. This relationship is a complex one, however, in that it is probably not personality alone, but the way in which it combines with other factors that contributes to second language learning.

Motivation and attitudes

There has been a great deal of research on the role of attitudes and motivation in second language learning. The overall findings show that positive attitudes and motivation are related to success in second language learning (Gardner 1985). Unfortunately, the research cannot indicate precisely *how* motivation affects learning. That is, we do not know whether it is the motivation that produces successful learning or successful learning that enhances motivation. Are learners more highly motivated because they are successful, or are they successful because they are highly motivated? (Skehan 1989)

Motivation in second language learning is a complex phenomenon which can be defined in terms of two factors: learners' communicative needs, and their attitudes towards the second language community. If learners need to speak the second language in a wide range of social situations or to fulfil professional ambitions, they will perceive the communicative value of the second language and will therefore be motivated to acquire proficiency in it. Likewise, if learners have favourable attitudes towards the speakers of the language, they will desire more contact with them. On the other hand, we should keep in mind that an individual's identity is closely linked with the way he or she speaks. It follows that when speaking a new language, one is adopting some of the identity markers of another cultural group. Depending on the learner's attitudes, learning a second language can be a source of enrichment or a source of resentment. If the speaker's only reason for learning the second language is external pressure, internal motivation may be minimal and general attitudes towards learning may be negative.

One factor which often affects motivation is the social dynamic or power relationship between the languages. That is, members of a minority group may have different attitudes and motivation when learning the language of a majority group than those of majority group members learning a minority language. Even though it is impossible to predict the exact effect of such societal factors on second language learning, the fact that languages exist in social contexts cannot be overlooked when we seek to understand the variables which affect success in learning. Even children are sensitive to social dynamics and power relationships.

Learning styles

An area of research which has received a lot of attention in many areas of education is the issue of learning styles. This research suggests that different learners approach a task with a different set of skills and preferred strategies. We have all heard people say that they cannot learn something until they have seen it. Such learners would fall into the group called 'visual' learners. Other people, who may be called 'aural' learners, seem to need only to hear something once or twice before they know it. Some learners feel compelled to memorize and will practise and practise until they have committed new information to memory, before they feel comfortable that they have a grasp of it. For still others, there is a need to add physical action to the learning process. It is not enough to see, hear, or practise for these learners. They need to live the new knowledge in ways that involve them more completely.

Of course, all of us learn in all these ways. We can all benefit from a variety of learning experiences. However, there is clearly some truth to the intuition that certain ways of approaching a task are more successful for one person than for another, and that when learners are given some freedom to choose their preferred way of learning, they will do better than those who find themselves forced to learn in environments where a learning style which does not suit them is imposed as the only way to learn.

Apart from Reid (1987), there is very little research on the interaction between different learning styles and success in second language acquisition. Nevertheless, the research which has been carried out, on SLA and in other fields, tells us that when learners express a preference for seeing something written, or want to memorize material which we feel should be learned in a less formal way, we should not assume that their ways of working are wrong. Instead, we should encourage them to use all means available to them as they work to learn another language (Oxford 1990).

At a minimum, research on learning styles should make us sceptical of claims that a particular teaching method or textbook will suit the needs of all learners.

Age of acquisition

We now turn to a learner characteristic of a different type: age. This is a characteristic which is easier to define and measure than personality, aptitude, or motivation. Nevertheless, the relationship between a learner's age and his or her potential for success in second language acquisition is the subject of much lively debate.

It has been widely observed that children from immigrant families eventually speak the language of their new community with native-like fluency.

Their parents rarely achieve such high levels of mastery of the new language. Adult second language learners may become very capable of communicating successfully in the language, but there will always be differences of accent, word choice, or grammatical features which set them apart from native speakers or from speakers who began learning the language while they were very young.

One explanation for this difference is that, as in first language acquisition, there is a critical period for second language acquisition. As discussed in Chapter 2, the Critical Period Hypothesis suggests that there is a time in human development when the brain is predisposed for success in language learning. Developmental changes in the brain, it is argued, change the nature of second language acquisition. According to this view, language learning which occurs after the end of the critical period may not be based on the innate structures believed to contribute to first language acquisition or second language acquisition in early childhood. Rather, older learners depend on more general learning abilities—the same ones they might use to learn other kinds of skills or information. It is argued that these general learning abilities are not as successful for language learning as the more specific, innate capacities which are available to the young child. It is most often claimed that the critical period ends somewhere around puberty, and that adolescents and adults are no longer able to call upon the innate language acquisition capacities which work so well for young children.

Of course, as we saw in Chapter 2, it is difficult to compare children and adults as second language learners. One of the difficulties in making the comparison is that the conditions for language learning are often very different. Younger learners in informal language learning environments usually have more time to devote to learning language. They often have more opportunities to hear and use the language in environments where they do not experience strong pressure to speak fluently and accurately from the very beginning. Furthermore, their early imperfect efforts are often praised or, at least, accepted. On the other hand, older learners are often in situations which demand much more complex language and the expression of much more complicated ideas. Adults are often embarrassed by their lack of mastery of the language and they may develop a sense of inadequacy after experiences of frustration in trying to say exactly what they mean.

The critical period hypothesis has been challenged in recent years from several different points of view. Some studies of the second language development of older and younger learners who are learning in similar circumstances have shown that, at least in the early stages of second language development, older learners are more efficient than younger learners. In educational research, it has been reported that learners who began learning a second language at the primary school level did not fare better in the long run than those who began in early adolescence. Furthermore, there are countless anecdotes about older learners (adolescents and adults) who have reached high levels of proficiency in a second language. In neurological research, it has *not* been demonstrated that the hypothesized changes take place in the brain at puberty. Much research seems rather to suggest that the brains of very young infants already have some areas which are specialized for processing language.

In the following pages, we will review some of the important recent studies designed to investigate the critical period hypothesis as it relates to second language learning.

CPH: More than just accent?

Most studies which have investigated the relationship between age of acquisition and second language development have focused on learners' phonological (pronunciation) achievement. In general, these studies have concluded that older learners almost inevitably have a noticeable 'foreign accent'. But what of other linguistic features? Is syntax (word order, overall sentence structure) as dependent on age of acquisition as phonological development? Do older learners ever achieve native-like mastery of syntax? What about morphology (for example, grammatical endings which mark such things as verb tense or the number and gender of nouns)? One study that attempted to answer these questions is that of Mark Patkowski (1980).

Mastery of the spoken language

Mark Patkowski studied the effect of age on the acquisition of features of a second language other than accent. He hypothesized that, even if accent were ignored, only those who had begun learning their second language before the age of 15 could ever achieve full, native-like mastery of that language. Patkowski examined the spoken English of 67 highly educated immigrants to the United States. They had started to learn English at various ages, but all had lived in the United States for more than five years. The spoken English of 15 native-born Americans from a similarly high level of education was also examined. Their speech served as a sort of baseline of what the second language learners might be trying to attain as the target language. Inclusion of the native speakers also provided evidence concerning the validity of the research procedures. A lengthy interview with each of the subjects in the study was tape recorded.

Because Patkowski wanted to remove the possibility that the results would be affected by accent, he did not ask the raters to judge the tape-recorded interviews themselves. Instead, he transcribed five-minute samples from the interviews. These samples (from which any identifying or revealing information about immigration history had been removed) were rated by trained native-speaker judges. The judges were asked to place each speaker on a rating scale from 0, representing no knowledge of the language, and 5, representing a level of English expected from an educated native speaker.

The main question in Patkowski's research was: 'Will there be a difference between learners who began to learn English before puberty and those who began learning English later?' However, in the light of some of the issues discussed above, he also compared learners on the basis of other characteristics and experiences which some people have suggested might be as good as age in predicting or explaining a learner's eventual success in mastering a second language. For example, he looked at the relationship between eventual mastery and the total amount of time a speaker had been in the United States as well as the amount of formal ESL instruction the learner had had.

The findings were quite dramatic. Thirty-two out of 33 subjects who had begun learning English before the age of fifteen scored at the 4+ or the 5 level. The homogeneity of the pre-puberty learners seemed to suggest that, for this group, success in learning a second language was almost inevitable (see Figure 3.1). On the other hand, there was much more variety in the levels achieved by the post-puberty group. The majority of the post-puberty learners centred around the 3+ level, but there was a distribution of levels (see Figure 3.1). This variety made the performance of this group look more like the sort of performance range one would expect if one were measuring success in learning almost any kind of skill or knowledge.

Patkowski's first question, 'Will there be a difference between learners who began to learn English before puberty and those who began learning English later?', was answered with a very resounding 'yes'. When he examined the other factors which might be thought to affect success in second language acquisition, the picture was much less clear. There was, naturally, some relationship between these other factors and learning success. However, it often turned out that age was so closely related to the other factors that it was not really possible to separate them completely. For example, length of residence in the United States sometimes seemed to be a fairly good predictor. However, while it was true that a person who had lived in the country for fifteen years might speak better than one who had been there for only ten years, it was often the case that the one with longer residence had also arrived at an earlier age. However, a person who had arrived in the United States at the age of eighteen and had lived there for twenty years did not score significantly better than someone who had arrived at the age of eighteen but had only lived there for ten years. Similarly, amount of instruction, when separated from age, did not predict success to the extent that age of immigration did.

Thus, Patkowski found that age of acquisition is a very important factor in setting limits on the development of native-like mastery of a second

Figure 3.1: Bar charts showing the language levels of pre- and post-puberty learners of English (Patkowski 1980).

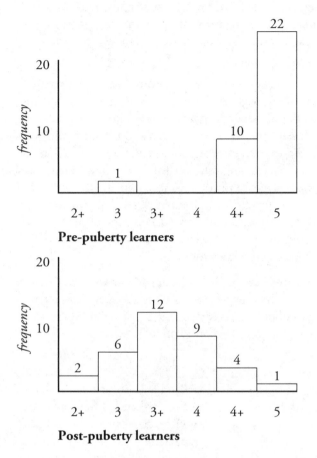

language and that this limitation does not apply only to accent. These results gave added support to the critical period hypothesis for second language acquisition.

Experience and research have shown that native-like mastery of the spoken language is difficult to attain by older learners. Surprisingly, even the ability to distinguish between grammatical and ungrammatical sentences in a second language appears to be affected by the age factor, as we will see in the next study by Newport and Johnson.

Intuitions of grammaticality

Jacqueline Johnson and Elissa Newport conducted a study of 46 Chinese and Korean speakers who had begun to learn English at different ages. All subjects were students or faculty at an American university and all had been in the United States for at least three years. The study also included 23 native speakers of English (Johnson and Newport 1989).

The participants in the study were given a *grammaticality judgement* task which tested twelve rules of English morphology and syntax (verb tense, noun pluralization, verb agreement, word order, question formation, use of articles, and use of pronouns). They heard sentences on a tape and had to indicate whether or not each sentence was correct. Half of the sentences were grammatical, half were not.

When they scored the tests, Johnson and Newport found that age of arrival was a significant predictor of success on the test. When they grouped the learners in the same way as Patkowski, comparing those who began their intensive exposure to English between the ages of three and fifteen with those who arrived in the United States between the ages of seventeen and 39, once again they found that there was a strong relationship between an early start to language learning and performance in the second language. Johnson and Newport noted that before the age of fifteen, and especially before the age of ten, there are few individual differences in second language ability. Older learners will not have native-like language skills and are more likely to differ greatly from one another in ultimate attainment.

This study, then, further supports the hypothesis that there is a critical period for attaining full native-like mastery of a second language. Nevertheless, there is some research which suggests that older learners may have an advantage, at least in the early stages of second language learning.

Is younger really better?

In 1978, Catherine Snow and Marian Hoefnagel-Höhle published an article based on a research project they had carried out in Holland. They had studied the progress of a group of English speakers who were learning Dutch as a second language. What made their research especially valuable was that the learners they were following included children as young as three years old as well as adolescents and adults. Furthermore, a large number of different types of language use and language knowledge were measured and analysed.

Pronunciation was tested by having learners pronounce 80 Dutch words twice: the first time immediately after hearing a native speaker say the word; the second time, a few minutes later, they were asked to say the word represented in a picture, without a model to imitate. Tape recordings of the learners were rated by a native speaker of Dutch on a six-point scale.

In an *auditory discrimination* test, learners saw pictures of four objects. In each group of four there were two whose names were minimal pairs, that is, alike except for one sound (an example in English would be 'ship' and 'sheep'). Learners heard one of the words and were asked to indicate which picture was named by the word they heard.

Morphology was tested using a procedure which required learners to complete sentences by adding the correct grammatical markers to words which were supplied by the researchers. Again, to take an example from English, learners were asked to complete sentences such as 'Here is one boy. Now there are two of them. There are two _____ .'

The *sentence repetition task* required learners to repeat 37 sentences of increasing length and grammatical complexity.

For *sentence translation*, learners were given 60 sentences to translate from English to Dutch. A point was given for each grammatical structure which was rendered into the correct Dutch equivalent.

In the *sentence judgement task*, learners were to judge which of two sentences was better. The same content was expressed in both sentences, but one sentence was grammatically correct while the other contained errors.

In the *Peabody Picture Vocabulary Test*, learners saw four pictures and heard one isolated word. Their task was to indicate which picture corresponds to the word spoken by the tester.

For the *story comprehension task*, learners heard a story in Dutch and were then asked to retell the story in English or Dutch (according to their preference).

Finally, the *storytelling task* required learners to tell a story which corresponded to a set of pictures they were given. Rate of delivery of speech mattered more than the expression of content or formal accuracy.

The learners were divided into several age groups, but for our discussion we will divide them into just three groups: children (aged 3 to 10), adolescents (12 to 15 years), and adults (18 to 60 years). The children and adolescents all attended Dutch schools. Some of the adults worked in Dutch work environments, but most of their Dutch colleagues spoke English well. Other adults were parents who did not work outside their homes and thus had somewhat less contact with Dutch than most of the other subjects.

The learners were tested three times, at four- to five-month intervals. They were first tested within six months of their arrival in Holland and within six weeks of their starting school or work in a Dutch language environment.

Activity
Which group do you think did best on the first test (that is, who learned *fastest*)? Which group do you think was best by the end of the year? Do you think some groups would do better on certain tasks than others? For example, who do you think would do best on the pronunciation tasks, and who would do best on the tasks requiring more metalinguistic awareness? Compare your predictions with the results on the different tasks which are presented in Table 3.1. An 'X' indicates that the group was best on this test at the beginning of the year (an indication of the rate of learning), and a 'Y'

indicates the group that did best at the end of the year (an indication of eventual attainment).

Table 3.1: Comparison of language learning at different ages

Task	Child	Adolescent	Adult
Pronunciation	Y	Y	X
Auditory discrimination		XY	
Morphology		XY	
Sentence repetition		XY	
Sentence translation	*	XY	
Sentence judgement	*	XY	
Peabody picture vocabulary test		XY	
Story comprehension	Y	X	
Storytelling	Y	X	

* These tests were too difficult for child learners.

In the Snow and Hoefnagel-Höhle study, the adolescents were by far the most successful learners. They were ahead of everyone on all but one of the tests (pronunciation) on the first test session. That is, within the first few months the adolescents had already made the most progress in learning Dutch. As the table indicates, it was the adults who were better than the children and adolescents on the pronunciation test at the first test session. Surprisingly, it was also the adults, not the children, whose scores were second best on the other tests at the first test session. In other words, adolescents and adults learned faster than children in the first few months of exposure to Dutch.

By the end of the year, however, the children were rapidly catching up or had, in fact, surpassed the adults on several measures (for example, pronunciation, story comprehension, and storytelling). Nevertheless, it was the adolescents who retained the highest levels of performance overall.

Snow and Hoefnagel-Höhle concluded that their results provide evidence that there is no critical period for language acquisition. However, their results can be interpreted in different ways as well:

1 Some of the tasks, for example, sentence judgement or translation, were too hard for young learners. They were simply beyond the children's *cognitive* capacities.

2 While adults and adolescents learn faster in the early stages of second

language development, young children eventually catch up and even surpass them if their exposure to the language takes place in contexts where they are surrounded by the language on a daily basis. In other words, adults and adolescents learn at a faster *rate*, while children surpass adults and adolescents in *eventual attainment.*

3 Adults and adolescents can make considerable and rapid progress towards mastery of a second language in contexts where they can make use of the language on a daily basis in social, personal, professional, or academic interaction.

At what age should second language instruction begin?

After reading the critical period studies, it is tempting to say, 'I didn't start studying a second language in childhood, so what's the point of trying?' or, 'If second language teaching programs are to succeed, they had better begin with very young children'. However, we know that even if native-like mastery of a second language is usually not possible for learners who begin learning later in life, experience and research both show that older learners are able to attain high levels of proficiency in their second language. Furthermore, it is essential to think carefully about the goals of an instructional program and the context in which it occurs before we jump to conclusions about the necessity—or even the desirability—of the earliest possible start.

The role of the critical period in second language acquisition is still a much debated topic. For every researcher who holds that there are maturational constraints on language acquisition, there is another who considers that the age factor cannot be separated from factors such as motivation, social identity, and the conditions for learning. They argue that older learners may well speak with an accent because they want to continue being identified with their first language cultural group. And adults rarely get access to the same quantity and quality of language input that children receive in play settings.

Many people conclude on the basis of studies such as those by Patkowski, and Newport and Johnson that it is better to begin second language instruction as early as possible. Yet it is very important to bear in mind the context of these studies. They deal with the highest possible level of second language skills, the level at which a second language speaker is indistinguishable from a native speaker. But achieving a native-like mastery of the second language is not a goal for all second language learning, in all contexts.

When the objective of second language learning is native-like mastery of the target language, it is usually desirable for the learner to be completely surrounded by the language as early as possible. However, in the case of children from minority language backgrounds or homes where language, literacy, and education are not well-developed, early intensive exposure to the second language may entail the loss or incomplete development of the child's first language. This leads to so-called *subtractive bilingualism*, where one language is lost before another is fully developed. Subtractive bilingualism may, in turn, lead to academic and personal problems. For these children, programs promoting the development of their first language at home and at school can help to prevent some of these problems. Such programs allow children to continue to use their stronger first language while they learn the second language. This encouragement of the first language can have positive effects on the children's self-esteem, on their relationships with their parents, on their early cognitive development, and somewhat paradoxically, on their eventual mastery of the second language.

When the goal is basic communicative ability for all students in a school setting, and when it is assumed that the child's native language will remain the primary language, it may be more efficient to begin second language teaching later. In research on school learners receiving a few hours of instruction per week, learners who start later (for example, at age 10, 11, or 12) catch up very quickly with those who began earlier. Any school program should be based on realistic estimates of how long it takes to learn a second language. One or two hours a week – even for seven or eight years – will not produce very advanced second language speakers.

The learner's age is one of the characteristics which determine the way in which an individual approaches second language learning. But the opportunities for learning (both inside and outside the classroom), the motivation to learn, and individual differences in aptitude for language learning are also important determining factors in both rate of learning and eventual success in learning.

Summary

In this chapter, we have looked at the ways in which intelligence, aptitude, personality and motivational characteristics, learning styles, and age have been found to influence second language learning. We have learned that the study of individual learner variables is not easy and that the results of research are not entirely satisfactory. This is partly because of the lack of clear definitions and methods for measuring the individual characteristics. It is also due to the fact that these learner characteristics are not independent of one another: learner variables interact in complex ways. So far, researchers know very little about the nature of these complex interactions. Furthermore, in a classroom, a sensitive teacher, who takes learners' individual personalities and learning styles into account, can create a learning environment in which virtually all learners can be successful in learning a second language. Therefore, it remains difficult to make precise predictions about how a particular individual's characteristics influence his or her success as a language learner.

Sources and suggestions for further reading

General discussion of individual differences

Skehan, P. 1989. *Individual Differences in Second Language Learning.* London: Edward Arnold.

Intelligence

Genesee, F. 1976. 'The role of intelligence in second language learning.' *Language Learning* 26: 267–80.

Aptitude

Wesche, M.B. 1981. 'Language aptitude measures in streaming, matching students with methods, and diagnosis of learning problems' in K. Diller (ed.): *Individual Differences and Universals in Language Learning Aptitude.* Rowley, Mass.: Newbury House. pp. 119–39.

The case of CJ

Obler, L. 1989. 'Exceptional second language learners' in S. Gass, C. Madden, D. Preston, and L. Selinker (eds.): *Variation in Second Language Acquisition, Vol. II: Psycholinguistic Issues.* Clevedon, UK/Philadelphia, Pa.: Multilingual Matters. pp. 141–59.

Motivation and attitudes

Gardner, R. 1985. *Social Psychology and Second Language Learning: The Role of Attitudes and Motivation.* London: Edward Arnold.

Inhibition and second language learning

Guiora, A., B. Beit-Hallahmi, R. Brannon, C. Dull, and **T. Scovel.** 1972. 'The effects of experimentally induced changes in ego states on pronunciation ability in a second language: An exploratory study.' *Comprehensive Psychiatry* 13: 139–50.

Learning styles and learner strategies

Reid, J. 1987. 'The learning style preferences of ESL students.' *TESOL Quarterly* 21/1: 87–111.

Oxford, R. 1990. *Language Learning Strategies: What Every Teacher Should Know.* New York: Newbury House.

Age of acquisition

Johnson, J., and **E. Newport.** 1989. 'Critical period effects in second language learning: The influence of maturational state on the acquisition of English as a Second Language.' *Cognitive Psychology* 21: 60–99.

Long, M. H. 1990. 'Maturational constraints on language development.' *Studies in Second Language Acquisition* 12: 251–85.

Patkowski, M. 1980. 'The sensitive period for the acquisition of syntax in a second language.' *Language Learning* 30/2: 449–72.

Scovel, T. 1988. *A Time to Speak: A Psycholinguistic Inquiry into the Critical Period for Human Speech.* Cambridge, Mass.: Newbury House.

Snow, C. and **M. Hoefnagel-Höhle.** 1978. 'The critical period for language acquisition: Evidence from second language learning'. *Child Development* 49: 1114–28.

The importance of maintaining the first language

Cummins, J. 1984. *Bilingualism and Special Education: Issues in Assessment and Pedagogy.* Clevedon, UK: Multilingual Matters.

Wong-Fillmore, L. 1991. 'When learning a second language means losing the first.' *Early Childhood Research Quarterly* 6: 323–46.

LEARNER LANGUAGE

In this chapter we shift our attention away from learner characteristics to the learner's language itself. We examine the types of errors that learners make and discuss what their errors can tell us about their knowledge of the language and their ability to use that knowledge. We will also look at stages and sequences in the acquisition of particular linguistic forms, and discuss similarities and differences.

Knowing more about the development of learner language helps teachers to assess teaching procedures in the light of what they can reasonably expect to accomplish in the classroom. As we will see, there are some characteristics of learner language which can be quite perplexing if one does not have an overall picture of the steps learners go through in acquiring features of the second language.

In presenting some of the findings of SLA research, we have included a number of samples of learner language to illustrate the various research findings and to give you an opportunity to practise analysing learner language. Of course, teachers analyse learner language all the time, but their perspective is often that of measuring learner performance in terms of what has been taught. But progress cannot always be measured in these terms. Sometimes movement from one point in a sequence of development to another can actually lead from apparently correct performance (based on rote learning or formulaic speech) to incorrect performance (based on an emerging understanding of the underlying rules or grammatical relationships in the language they are learning). Thus, an increase in error is sometimes actually an indication of progress. A simple example of this is irregular verbs. Learners usually learn the irregular past tense forms of verbs before they learn the regular simple past -ed marker. That means that a learner who says 'I buyed a bus ticket' may know more about English than one who says 'I bought a bus ticket'.

The concept of learner language

As discussed in Chapter 1, children do not learn language simply through imitation and practice. Instead, as we saw, a large number of utterances produced by children are not like the utterances that they have heard, but seem to be based on some internal processes and knowledge which permit them to discover the complexities of the adult language gradually. Children's early speech seems best explained in terms of a developing system with its own interim rules, not simply as imitations of adult sentences.

Research on second language acquisition has shown that second language learners also pass through sequences of development. Many of these sequences are similar to those of children learning their first language. In addition, the features of a second language learner's previously learned languages will also influence the learner's developing second language system.

A number of studies have examined children's early language, not from the perspective of the adult's linguistic system, but in terms of its own characteristics. Children's earliest language is often called 'telegraphic'. At this early stage, children leave out many of the small words, like prepositions and articles, or inflections like the -*ed* marker for the past tense. It is called telegraphic because it is very much like the language adults use when they are sending telegrams and want to use just the essential words to convey the message economically.

Research has also shown that a child's knowledge of the grammatical system is built up in predictable sequences. For instance, grammatical markers such as the -*ing* of the present progressive or the -*ed* of the past tense are not acquired at the same time, but in sequence. Furthermore, the acquisition of certain grammatical features follows similar patterns in children in different environments. We will look at some details of this development later in this chapter. However, what is important to remember from the discussion so far is that child language is not viewed as an incorrect version of the adult system, but as a system in its own right. And as children continue to be exposed to opportunities to hear and use their language, they are able to revise these systems in ways which gradually develop towards the system of an adult.

But what about second language learning? Does it evolve in similar ways? Do second language learners develop their own language system in much the same way as first language learners? Until the late 1960s, most people regarded second language learners' speech as an incorrect version of the target language. This incorrect speech was considered to be largely a result of transfer from the learner's first language. Contrastive analysis was the basis for identifying differences between the first and second language and for predicting areas of potential error. So, for example, one might predict that a speaker of French would be likely to express the idea of being cold as 'I have cold' in English because this would be a direct translation of the way this meaning is expressed in French (*j'ai froid*).

As we saw in Chapter 2, however, not all errors made by second language learners could be explained in terms of first language transfer alone. A number of studies showed that many second language learners' errors could be explained better in terms of learners' attempts to discover the structure of the language being learned rather than an attempt to transfer patterns of their first language. Furthermore, some of the errors were remarkably similar to the kinds of errors made by young first language learners. An example would be the use of a regular *-ed* past tense ending on an irregular verb (for example, 'goed' instead of 'went').

As a result, a number of researchers began to take a different approach to analysing learners' errors. This approach, which developed during the 1970s, became known as 'error analysis' and involved a detailed description and analysis of the kinds of errors second language learners make. The goal of this research was to discover what learners really know about the language. This approach differed from contrastive analysis in that it did not set out to predict errors on the basis of interference from the mother tongue. Rather, it sought to discover and describe the different kinds of errors in an effort to understand how learners process the second language data. Error analysis was based on the assumption that the speech of second language learners is a system in its own right—one which is rule-governed and pre-dictable and very much like the system of young first language learners.

Larry Selinker gave the name *interlanguage* to learners' developing second language knowledge (Selinker 1972). Analysis of a learner's interlanguage shows that it has some characteristics of the learner's native language, some characteristics of the second language, and some characteristics which seem to be very general and tend to occur in all or most interlanguage systems. Interlanguages are systematic, but they are also dynamic, continually evolving as learners receive more input and revise their hypotheses about the second language. In the activity that follows, we will look at some of the different kinds of errors learners make.

Activity

The Great Toy Robbery

The following texts were written by two learners of English, one a French-speaking secondary school student, the other a Chinese-speaking adult learner. In both cases, the learners saw a cartoon film entitled *The Great Toy Robbery* (National Film Board of Canada). After viewing the film, students were asked to retell the story in writing.

Read the texts and examine the errors made by each learner. Do they make the same kinds of errors? In what ways do the two interlanguages differ?

Learner 1: French first language, secondary school student

> During a sunny day, a cowboy go in the desert with his horse. he has a big hat. His horse eat a flour. In the same time, Santa Clause go in a city to give some surprises. He has a red costume and a red packet of surprises. You have three robbers in the mountain who sees Santa Clause with a king of glaces that it permitted us to see at a long distance. Every robbers have a horse. They go in the way of Santa Clause, not Santa Clause but his pocket of surprises. After they will go in a city and they go in a saloon. [...]
> (Unpublished data from P. M. Lightbown and B. Barkman)

Learner 2: Chinese first language, adult

> This year Christmas comes soon! Santa Claus ride a one horse open sleigh to sent present for children. on the back of his body has big packet. it have a lot of toys. in the way he meet three robbers. They want to take his big packet. Santa Claus no way and no body help, so only a way give them, then three robbers ride their horse dashing through the town. There have saloon, they go to drink some beer and open the big packent. They plays toys in the Bar. They meet a cow boy in the saloon.
> (Unpublished data from M. J. Martens)

Many error types are common to both learners. Both make errors of subject-verb agreement (for example, 'a cowboy go' and 'three robbers in the mountain who sees' by Learner 1 and 'Santa Claus ride' and 'they plays' by Learner 2). Such errors are clearly not due to first language interference but rather are 'developmental' in nature. That is, they reflect learners' understanding of the second language system itself rather than an attempt to transfer characteristics of their first language. These are referred to as *developmental errors* because they are errors which might very well be made by children acquiring English as their first language. Sometimes these are errors of *overgeneralization*, that is, errors caused by trying to use a rule in a context where it does not belong, for example, a regular *-ed* ending on an irregular verb. Sometimes the errors are better described as *simplification*, where elements of a sentence are left out, for example, or where all verbs have the same form regardless of person, number, or tense.

One can also see, especially in Learner 2's text, the influence of classroom experience. An example is the use of formulaic expressions such as 'one horse open sleigh' which is taken verbatim from a well-known Christmas song which has no doubt been taught and sung in the learner's ESL class.

For those who are familiar with the English spoken by native speakers of French, some of the errors made by the first learner will readily be recognized as probably based on French. Similarly, those familiar with the English of Chinese speakers may recognize errors made by the Chinese learner as being due to the learner's attempt to use patterns of Chinese in English sentences. These are called *transfer* or 'interference' errors. It is clear, however, that it is very often difficult to determine the source of errors.

Developmental sequences

Research on language acquisition has revealed that there are important similarities between first language learners and second language learners. One important finding has been that, in both first and second language acquisition, there are sequences or 'stages' in the development of particular structures. That is, certain features of the language seem to appear relatively early in a learner's language while others are acquired much later. A somewhat surprising finding is that these *developmental sequences* are similar across learners from different backgrounds: what is learned early by one is learned early by others.

Among child language learners, this is perhaps not so unexpected because their language learning is partly tied to their cognitive development, that is, to their learning about the relationships among people, events, and objects around them. But among second language learners, whose experiences with the language may vary quite widely and whose cognitive development is essentially stable, it is more remarkable that developmental sequences are so similar. Furthermore, although learners obviously need to have opportunities to hear or read certain things before they begin to use them, it is not always the case that those features of the language which are most frequent are easiest to learn. For example, virtually every English sentence has one or more articles ('a' or 'the'), but many learners have great difficulty using these forms correctly. Finally, although there is some evidence that the learners' first language influences the sequences, many aspects of these developmental stages are similar among learners from many different first language backgrounds.

In the next section, the stages of acquisition for specific grammatical features are presented for first and second language learners.

Grammatical morphemes

First language acquisition

Much research has focused on how children develop inflections, like the third person singular -s or the past tense -ed, and function words such as the articles 'a' and 'the'. These small grammatical markers are sometimes referred to as *grammatical morphemes*.

One of the best-known studies which investigated the development of grammatical morphemes in child first language development was carried out by Roger Brown in the late 1960s and early 1970s. He studied how three children (Adam, Eve, and Sarah) learned fourteen of these morphemes over time, and found that they acquired them in a remarkably similar sequence (Brown 1973). The list below is a somewhat simplified version of the grammatical morphemes studied by Roger Brown. They are listed in the approximate order of their acquisition by children learning English as their mother tongue.

> present progressive -*ing* (Mommy runn*ing*)
> plural -*s* (two book*s*)
> irregular past forms (Baby *went*)
> possessive '*s* (daddy'*s* hat)
> copula (Annie *is* a nice girl)
> articles 'the' and 'a'
> regular past -*ed* (She walk*ed*)
> third person singular simple present -*s* (She run*s*)
> auxiliary 'be' (He *is* coming)

A child who had mastered the grammatical morphemes at the bottom of the list was sure to have mastered those at the top of the list, but the reverse was not true. Thus, Brown could claim there was evidence for a sequence or *order of acquisition*. The children mastered the morphemes at different rates, however. For example, Eve had mastered nearly all the morphemes before she was two years old while Sarah was nearly four before she reached the same level. The study carried out by Brown was a *longitudinal* study, that is, he studied the same learners over a period of time.

In other first language morpheme acquisition research, Jill and Peter de Villiers did a *cross-sectional* study (1973). This means that they studied a large group of children who were at different ages and stages of development. They found that children who correctly used the morphemes which Adam, Eve, and Sarah had acquired late were also correct in using the ones which Adam, Eve, and Sarah had acquired earlier. Those children who accurately used the 'early' morphemes, however, had not necessarily mastered the 'late' ones. The children mastered the morphemes at different ages, just as Adam, Eve, and Sarah had done, but the *order* of their acquisition was very similar. These children were similar to each other *and* similar to Adam, Eve, and Sarah.

Second language acquisition in natural settings

Several studies to examine the development of grammatical morphemes have been carried out with learners who have learned English as a second language in a natural (non-instructional) environment.

The researchers took samples from a large number of learners at one point in time, scored each morpheme for accuracy in the learners' speech, and came up with an *accuracy order* for the morphemes. These studies were done with learners of different ages and from different first language backgrounds.

The overall results of the studies revealed an order which, while not the same as that found in the first language studies, was similar among learners from different first language backgrounds. This suggests that natural second language learners acquire grammatical morphemes in much the same way that first language learners do and that this natural sequence is not determined only or even mainly by the learner's first language.

Although a review of all the 'morpheme acquisition' studies suggests that the learner's first language has a more important influence on acquisition orders than some researchers would claim, there are some very strong patterns of similarity which cannot be explained by the influence of the first language.

There are still some unanswered questions in the morpheme acquisition literature. Just how much variation in this order is due to mother-tongue influence, the situation in which the learner language is observed, or individual learner factors, remains somewhat controversial. Nonetheless, it does seem as if second language learners tend to acquire a set of English grammatical morphemes in a similar order (see Larsen-Freeman and Long 1991).

Negative sentences

First language acquisition

Children learn the functions of negation very early. That is, they learn to deny, reject, disagree with, and refuse something by using the negative without too much trouble. However, even though they have this awareness of how negation functions, it takes some time before they have learned the grammatical rules to express the variety of negative functions (see Bloom and Lahey 1978).

Stage 1
The child's first negatives usually consist of the word 'no', which is simply tagged onto a word or phrase, either at the beginning or at the end:

> No go. No cookie. No comb hair.

Some children even adopt the word 'any' as a negator:

> Any bath!

Stage 2
At this stage, the negative element is inserted into a more complex sentence. Children may add forms of the negative other than *no*. However, they do not yet vary these forms for different persons or tenses:

I can't do it. He don't want it.

Stage 3
Later, children begin to produce the correct form of the verbs 'do', 'be', and modal verbs such as 'can' to suit the person, number, and tense:

You didn't have supper. She doesn't want it.

Second language acquisition in natural settings

Research on second language acquisition has revealed that learners pass through stages of acquisition which are very similar to those of first language learners. This does not mean that there are no differences due to the learners' native language, but the differences are less striking than the similarities. (See Schumann 1979 for a review of research on negation in second language learning.)

Stage 1
The negative element (usually 'no' or 'not') is typically placed before the verb or the element being negated:

No bicycle. No have any sand. I not like it.

'No' is preferred by some learners, perhaps due to transfer from their first language. Italian and Spanish speakers may prefer 'no' since it corresponds to the negative form in Italian and Spanish.

Stage 2
At this stage, 'no' and 'not' are alternated with 'don't'. However, 'don't' is not marked for person, number or tense and it may even be used before modals like 'can' and 'should':

He don't like it. I don't can sing.

Stage 3
Learners begin to place the negative element after auxiliary verbs like 'are', 'is', and 'can'. But at this stage, the 'don't' form is still not fully analysed:

You can't go there. He can't eat nothing. She don't like rice.

Stage 4
'Do' performs its full function as a marker of tense and person:

It doesn't work. We didn't have supper.

For some time, however, learners may continue to mark tense, person, and number on both the auxiliary and the verb:

I didn't went there. She doesn't wants to go.

Question formation

First language acquisition

There is a remarkable consistency as well in the way children learn to form questions in English. For one thing, there is a predictable order in which the '*wh*- words' emerge (see Bloom and Lahey 1978).

'What' is generally the first *wh*- question word to be used. It is often learned as part of a whole ('Whatsat?' or 'Whatsit?') and it is some time before the child learns that there are variations of the form, such as 'What is that?' and 'What are these?'

'Where' and 'who' emerge very soon, reflecting the fact that the child can only ask what he or she can already answer, questions about the here and now. This is reinforced by the fact that adults tend to ask children just these types of questions in the early days of language learning.

'Why' emerges around the end of the second year and becomes a favourite for the next year or two! Children seem to make an endless number of questions beginning with 'why'. At this age, the child does not really have a very good understanding of the meaning of the word, but has clearly discovered the usefulness of this little word in getting adults to engage in conversation.

Finally, when the child begins to understand manner and time, 'how' and 'when' emerge. In contrast to 'what', 'where', and 'who' questions, children sometimes ask the more cognitively difficult 'why', 'when', and 'how' questions without fully understanding their meaning.

Since the developing use of these question words is at least partly tied to children's cognitive development and to the types of questions which children are asked, it is perhaps not surprising that there is this consistency in the sequence of their acquisition. Perhaps more remarkable is the consistency in the acquisition of word order in questions. This development is not based on learning new meanings, but rather on learning different linguistic forms to express meanings which are already clear—both to the child and to the interlocutor.

Stage 1

Children's earliest questions are single words or simple two- or three-word sentences with rising intonation:

Cookie? Mommy book?

At the same time, of course, they may produce some correct questions—correct because they have been learned as formulaic 'chunks':

Where's Daddy? What's that?

Stage 2

When their sentences grow longer, children produce questions without changing the internal structure of the sentence. With 'yes/no' questions, they simply add rising intonation. With *wh*-questions, they put a question word at the beginning:

> You like this? I have some? Why you catch it?

At this stage, they may continue to produce the correct 'chunk-learned' form:

> What's that?

Stage 3

Gradually, they notice that the structure of questions is different and begin to produce questions such as:

> Can I go? Is that mine?

But at this stage they may generalize that all questions are formed by putting a verb at the beginning of a sentence. Thus:

> Is the teddy is tired? Do I can have a cookie?

Furthermore, *wh-* questions usually retain the declarative word order:

> Why you don't have one?

At this stage the children seem to have worked out that, in a question, some element must appear at the beginning of the sentence, but they are not yet aware that there must also be some change in the word order of the sentence itself. We can call this stage 'fronting' because the children place some sort of question marker—an auxiliary verb or a *wh-* word—at the front of the sentence, but they do not change the order of the elements within the sentence.

Stage 4

Later, children begin to master the use of the inversion and can even add 'do' in sentences in which no auxiliary would be required for the declarative version of the sentence:

> Do you like ice cream?

Some *wh-* questions, especially those which were learned early as formulaic expressions, seem to have inversion, but inversion is not used with all auxiliary verbs at this point in development:

> What's that? Where's the big one?

Even at this stage, however, it sometimes seems that they can either use inversion or use a *wh-*word, but not both. Therefore, we may find inversion in 'yes/no' questions but not in *wh-* questions:

> Can he eat the cookie? Where I can draw them?

Stage 5

Eventually, children combine both operations:

> Why can he go out?

However, it may still be beyond their ability to carry out a third or fourth operation, for example to negate the question as well as invert it:

> Why he can't go out?

Stage 6

Finally, when performance on questions is correct and well-established, there is still one more hurdle. When *wh-* words appear in subordinate clauses or embedded questions, children overgeneralize the inverted form and produce sentences such as:

> I don't know why can't he go out.

Figure 4.1: Developmental stages for question formation (adapted from Pienemann, Johnston, and Brindley 1988)

Stage 1	**Single words or formulae**	'Four children?'
Stage 2	**Declarative word order** no inversion, no fronting:	'It's a monster in the right corner?' 'The boys throw the shoes?'
Stage 3	**Fronting:** *wh-*fronting, no inversion:	'Where the little children are?' 'What's the dog are playing?'
	*do-*fronting:	'Do you have a shoes on your picture?' 'Does in this picture there is four astronauts?'
	other-fronting:	'Is the picture has two planets on top?'
Stage 4	**Inversion in *wh-* and 'yes/no' questions** copula in *wh-* questions:	'Where is the sun?'
	auxiliary other than 'do' in 'yes/no' questions:	'Is there fish in the water?'
Stage 5	**Inversion in *wh-* questions** inverted *wh-* questions with 'do':	'How do you say [proche]?'
	inverted *wh-* questions with auxiliaries other than 'do':	'What's the boy doing?'
Stage 6	**Complex questions** question tag: negative question: embedded question:	'It's better, isn't it?' 'Why can't you go?' 'Can you tell me what the date is today?'

Second language acquisition in natural settings

Manfred Pienemann and his colleagues have developed a framework for describing second language question stages for learners from a variety of first language backgrounds (Pienemann, Johnston, and Brindley 1988). An adapted version of the stages is shown in Figure 4.1.

It is clear from this figure that second language learners learn to form questions in a sequence of development which is similar in most respects to first language question development. There are also differences which seem to be due to the influence of previously learned languages as well as other individual factors. What is perhaps most striking however, is that even learners whose first language has subject-auxiliary inversion for questions go through a phase of using declarative word order and a period of 'fronting' in forming questions in their second language.

Activity

Learners' questions

The questions below were asked by students in a grade 5 intensive English class in Quebec, Canada. The children (aged 10–12) are all French-speaking and have little contact with English outside their English class. In their English classes they spend most of their time in communicative activity, and their teachers rarely correct their errors or focus on specific points of grammar. In many ways, these students have an experience of their second language which is similar to that of learners in a natural setting.

These questions were recorded while the children were playing a picture identification game. Their interlocutor was looking at a picture which was a duplicate of *one* of the four pictures which the students could see. The children asked these questions in order to gather information which would permit them to guess which picture the interlocutor was holding.

Based on the information in Figure 4.1, can you identify which stage of second language question development each question fits into?

Learner 1	Stage					
1 Does a dog is black and white?	1	2	3	4	5	6
2 Where the dog is?	1	2	3	4	5	6
3 It is five questions?	1	2	3	4	5	6
Learner 2						
4 Does the dog has a little spot black?	1	2	3	4	5	6
5 Where is the astronaut?	1	2	3	4	5	6
6 Does the ball is on the air?	1	2	3	4	5	6
Learner 3						
7 What is the dog doing?	1	2	3	4	5	6
8 Is the boy point the dog?	1	2	3	4	5	6
9 Is the shoe on the grass?	1	2	3	4	5	6

Answer Key

Learner 1: Questions 1 and 2 are stage 3: 'does' and 'where' appear simply to be 'fronted' to form a question. Question 3 is stage 2: there has been no adjustment to the word order of a declarative sentence; only the rising intonation identifies the sentence as a question.

Learner 2: Questions 4 and 6 are stage 3: again, 'does' seems simply to have been placed at the front of the sentence. Question 5 appears to be a stage 4 question: apparent inversion, but only with the verb 'be' used as a copula (linking verb).

Learner 3: Question 7 is stage 5: a *wh-* question with both inversion of the subject and the auxiliary and the second verb ('doing') placed correctly after the subject. Questions 8 and 9 are stage 4: correct subject-verb inversion in 'yes/no' questions.

Relative clauses

A number of studies have found that second language learners first acquire relative clauses in the subject and direct object positions, and only later (and in some cases, never) learn to use them to modify nouns in other sentence roles (for example, indirect object and object of preposition).

A summary of the observed pattern of acquisition for relative clauses is shown in Table 4.1 overleaf. It is referred to as the 'accessibility hierarchy' because it reflects the apparent ease with which learners have 'access' to certain structures in the target language.

Unlike the study of grammatical morphemes, negation, and questions, the study of relative clauses has not been principally inspired by research on child language. The hierarchy was first described in a study of languages of the world. Edward Keenan and Bernard Comrie (1977) found that languages which included the structures at the bottom of this list would also have those at the top, but the opposite was not true. Research on this aspect of second language development has shown that if a learner can use one of the structures at the bottom of the list, he or she will probably be able to use any that precede it (see, for example, Doughty 1991). On the other hand, a learner who can produce sentences with relative clauses in the subject or direct object positions will not necessarily be able to use relatives in any other position.

Table 4.1: Accessibility hierarchy for relative clauses in English (adapted from Doughty 1991)

Part of speech	Relative clause
Subject	The girl who was sick went home.
Direct object	The girl who I saw was pretty.
Indirect object	The girl who I gave the present to was absent.
Object of preposition	I found the book that John was talking about.
Possessive	I know the girl whose father died.
Object of comparison	The person who John is taller than is Mary.

More about sequences of development

An important finding about developmental sequences is how they may interact with transfer from a learner's first language. For example, although it is true that all learners of English seem to pass through a stage of forming negative sentences by placing 'no' before the verb, some learners may stay longer in that stage than others. If a learner's native language forms the negative in just that way (for example, Spanish *No tienen muchos libros*, 'They don't have many books'), it may take longer for the learner to notice that native speakers of English do *not* form the negative in that way. Similarly, even though German requires subject-verb inversion to form questions (*Können sie tanzen?*, 'Can they dance?'), German learners of English will pass through a phase of asking questions without inversion. However, once they notice that English questions have subject-auxiliary inversion, they will tend to assume that subject-verb inversion is also possible. Thus, alongside correct questions such as 'Can I play?' one may hear questions such as 'Play you baseball?'.

This interaction between developmental sequences which are common to learners from many language backgrounds, and language features which are transferred from the learner's first language, illustrates how the learner uses a variety of sources of knowledge in the effort to learn the second language. Of course, in most cases, the learner is not even aware of making this 'effort'. It is simply the natural activity of the human mind.

Summary

We have seen in this chapter that in both first and second language acquisition there are systematic and predictable stages, or sequences, of acquisition. We have seen examples of this in the development of grammatical morphemes, negatives, questions, and relative clauses. It is important to emphasize, however, that stages are not like closed rooms. Learners do not leave one behind when they enter another. That is, in examining a language sample from an individual learner, one should not expect to find all and only examples of behaviours from one stage. On the contrary, at a given point in time, learners may use sentences typical of several different stages. It is perhaps better to think of a stage being characterized by the emergence and increasing frequency of a particular form rather than by the disappearance of an earlier one. Even when a more advanced stage comes to dominate in a learner's speech, conditions of stress or complexity in a communicative interaction can cause the learner to 'slip' back to an earlier stage.

The focus in this chapter has been on second language acquisition by people who, although they may receive some instruction, also have considerable exposure to their second language in natural settings—at work, in the schoolyard, in the supermarket, or the neighbourhood laundromat. In general, researchers have found that learners who receive grammar-based instruction still pass through the same developmental sequences and make the same types of errors as those who acquire language in natural settings. For example, in some of the most extensive work on acquisition sequences, Jürgen Meisel and his colleagues Manfred Pienemann and Harald Clahsen found very consistent patterns in the acquisition of German by speakers of several Romance languages who had little or no instruction in German as a second language (Meisel, Clahsen, and Pienemann 1981). Pienemann later found very similar patterns in the acquisition of German word order by speakers of English whose only exposure to the language was in their university German classes in Australia (Pienemann 1989). In the next chapter we will focus on second language learning in the classroom.

Sources and suggestions for further reading

General discussion of learner language

Cook, V. 1991. *Second Language Learning and Language Teaching*. London: Edward Arnold.

Ellis, R. 1986. *Understanding Second Language Acquisition.* Oxford: Oxford University Press.

Larsen-Freeman, D. and **M. H. Long.** 1991. *An Introduction to Second Language Acquisition Research.* New York: Longman.

Lightbown, P. M. 1985. 'Great expectations: Second language acquisition research and classroom teaching.' *Applied Linguistics* 6/2: 173–89.

The concept of interlanguage

Selinker, L. 1972. 'Interlanguage.' *IRAL* 10: 209–31.

Developmental stages in second language acquisition

Bloom, L. and **M. Lahey.** 1978. *Language Development and Language Disorders.* New York: John Wiley and Sons.

Brown, R. 1973. *A First Language: The Early Stages.* Cambridge, Mass.: Harvard University Press.

Doughty, C. 1991. 'Second language instruction does make a difference.' *Studies in Second Language Acquisition* 13/4: 431–69.

Meisel, J. M., H. Clahsen, and **M. Pienemann.** 1981. 'On determining developmental stages in natural second language acquisition.' *Studies in Second Language Acquisition* 3: 109–35.

Pienemann, M. 1989. 'Is language teachable? Psycholinguistic experiments and hypotheses.' *Applied Linguistics* 10/1: 52–79.

Pienemann, M., M. Johnston, and **G. Brindley.** 1988. 'Constructing an acquisition-based procedure for second language assessment.' *Studies in Second Language Acquisition* 10: 217–43.

Schumann, J. 1979. 'The acquisition of English negation by speakers of Spanish: a review of the literature' in R. W. Andersen (ed.): *The Acquisition and Use of Spanish and English as First and Second Languages.* Washington, D.C.: TESOL.

de Villiers, J. G. and **P. A. de Villiers.** 1973. 'A cross-sectional study of the acquisition of grammatical morphemes.' *Journal of Psycholinguistic Research* 2: 267–78.

Relative clause hierarchy

Keenan, E. and **B. Comrie.** 1977. 'Noun phrase accessibility and Universal Grammar.' *Linguistic Inquiry* 8: 63–99.

5 SECOND LANGUAGE LEARNING IN THE CLASSROOM

Comparing instructed and natural settings for language learning

Most people would agree that learning a second language in a natural acquisition context or 'on the street' is not the same as learning in the classroom. Many believe that learning 'on the street' is more effective. This belief may be based on the fact that most successful learners have had exposure to the language outside the classroom. What is special about natural language learning? Can we create the same environment in the classroom? Should we? Or are there essential contributions that only instruction—and not natural exposure—can provide?

In this chapter, we will look at five proposals which theorists have made for how second languages should be taught. We will review research on second language learning which has been carried out in classroom settings. This will permit us to explore further the way in which second language research and theory contribute to our understanding of the advantages and the limitations of different approaches to second language teaching.

Before we go further, let us take a moment to reflect on the differences between natural and instructional language learning settings. We will then look at transcripts from two classrooms and try to understand what principles guide the teacher in each case.

Activity

Natural and instructional settings

The chart in Table 5.1 (page 71) is similar to Table 2.1 in Chapter 2 (page 21), in which we compared the profiles of first and second language learners. Think about the characteristics of the different contexts for second language learning.

Natural acquisition contexts should be understood as those in which the learner is exposed to the language at work or in social interaction or, if the learner is a child, in a school situation where most of the other children are native speakers of the target language and where the instruction is directed toward native speakers rather than toward learners of the language.

The traditional instruction environment is one where the language is being taught to a group of second or foreign language learners. In this case, the focus is on the language itself, rather than on information which is carried by the language. The teacher's goal is to see to it that students learn the vocabulary and grammatical rules of the target language. The goal of learners in such courses is often to pass an examination rather than to use the language for daily communicative interaction.

Communicative instruction environments also involve learners whose goal is learning the language itself, but the style of instruction places the emphasis on interaction, conversation, and language use, rather than on learning *about* the language. The topics which are discussed in the communicative instruction environment are often topics of general interest to the learner, for example, how to reply to a classified advertisement from a newspaper. Alternatively, the focus of a lesson may be on the subject matter, such as history or mathematics, which students are learning through the medium of the second language. In these classes, the focus may occasionally be on language itself, but the emphasis is on using the language rather than on talking about it. The language which teachers use for teaching is not selected on the basis of teaching a specific feature of the language, but on teaching learners to use the language in a variety of contexts. Students' success in these courses is often measured in terms of their ability to 'get things done' in the second language, rather than on their accuracy in using certain grammatical features.

In the chart below, mark a plus (+) if the characteristic in the left-hand column is typical of the learning environment in the three remaining columns. Mark a minus (–) if it is not something you usually find in that context. Write '?' if you are not sure.

Table 5.1: Comparison of natural and instructional settings

Characteristics	Natural acquisition	Traditional instruction	Communicative instruction
error correction			
learning one thing at a time			
ample time available for learning			
high ratio of native speakers to learners			
variety of language and discourse types			
pressure to speak			
access to modified input			

Photocopiable © Oxford University Press

As you look at the pattern of + and - signs you have placed in the chart, you will probably find it matches the following descriptions.

In natural acquisition settings
– Learners are rarely corrected. If their interlocutors can understand what they are saying, they do not remark on the correctness of the learners' speech. They would probably feel it was rude to do so.
– Language is not structured step by step. In communicative interactions, the learner will be exposed to a wide variety of vocabulary and structures.
– The learner is surrounded by the language for many hours each day. Some of it is addressed to the learner; much of it is simply 'overheard'.
– The learner encounters a number of different people who use the target language proficiently.
– The learner observes or participates in many different types of language events: brief greetings, commercial transactions, exchanges of information, arguments, instructions at school or in the workplace.
– Learners must often use their limited second language ability to respond to questions or get information. In these situations, the emphasis is on getting meaning across clearly, and more proficient speakers tend to be tolerant of errors that do not interfere with meaning.

- Modified input is available in many one-on-one conversations. In situations where many native speakers are involved in the conversation, however, the learner often has difficulty getting access to language he or she can understand.

Learners in traditional instruction
These differ from natural learners in that:
- Errors are frequently corrected. Accuracy tends to be given priority over meaningful interaction.
- Input is structurally simplified and sequenced. Linguistic items are presented and practised in isolation, one item at a time.
- There is limited time for learning (usually only a few hours a week).
- There is a small ratio of native speakers to non-native speakers. The teacher is often the only native or proficient speaker the student comes in contact with.
- Students experience a limited range of language discourse types (often a chain of 'Teacher asks a question/Student answers/Teacher evaluates response').
- Students often feel great pressure to speak or write the second language and to do so correctly from the very beginning.
- When teachers use the target language to give instructions or in other classroom management events, they often modify their language in order to ensure comprehension and compliance.

Not all language classrooms are alike. The conditions for learning differ in terms of the physical environment, the age and motivation of the students, the amount of time available for learning, and many other variables. Classrooms also differ in terms of the principles which guide teachers in their language teaching methods and techniques. The design of communicative language teaching programs has sought to replace some of the characteristics of traditional instruction with those more typical of natural acquisition contexts.

Communicative language teaching classrooms
Thus, in communicative language teaching classrooms we may find the following characteristics:
- There is a limited amount of error correction, and meaning is emphasized over form.
- Input is simplified and made comprehensible by the use of contextual cues, props, and gestures, rather than through *structural grading* (the presentation of one grammatical item at a time, in a sequence of 'simple' to 'complex').
- Learners usually have only limited time for learning. Sometimes, however, subject-matter courses taught through the second language can add time for language learning.
- Contact with proficient or native speakers of the language is limited. As

with traditional instruction, it is often only the teacher who is a proficient speaker. In communicative classrooms, learners have considerable exposure to the second language speech of other learners. This naturally contains errors which would not be heard in an environment where one's interlocutors are native speakers.

— A variety of discourse types are introduced through stories, role playing, the use of 'real-life' materials such as newspapers and television broadcasts, and field trips.

— There is little pressure to perform at high levels of accuracy, and there is often a greater emphasis on comprehension than on production in the early stages of learning.

— Modified input is a defining feature of this approach to instruction. The teacher in these classes makes every effort to speak to students in a level of language they can understand. In addition, other students speak a simplified language.

Activity

Classroom comparisons

In this activity we are going to look at transcripts from two classrooms, one using a traditional audiolingual, structure-based approach to teaching, and the other a communicative approach. *Audiolingual* teaching is based on the behaviourist theory of learning which places emphasis on forming habits and practising grammatical structures in isolation. The communicative approach, in contrast, is based on innatist and interactionist theories of language learning and emphasizes the communication of meaning. Grammatical forms are only focused on in order to clarify meaning. The theory is that learners can and must do the grammatical development on their own.

With each transcript, there is a little grid for you to check off whether certain things are happening in the interaction, from the point of view of the teacher and of the students. Before you begin reading the transcripts, study the following definitions of the categories used in the grids:

1 Errors	Are there errors in the language of either the teacher or the students?
2 Error correction	When grammatical errors are made, are they corrected? By whom?
3 Genuine questions	Do teachers and students ask questions to which they don't know the answer in advance?
4 Display questions	Do teachers and students ask questions they know the answers to so that learners can display knowledge (or the lack of it)?
5 Negotiation of meaning	Do the teachers and students work to understand what the other speakers are saying? What efforts are made by the teacher? By the students?

Teacher/student interactions

In the following excerpts, T represents the teacher; S represents a student. (The classroom examples in this chapter come from unpublished data collected by P. M. Lightbown, N. Spada, and B. Barkman.)

Classroom A: An audiolingual approach

(Students in this class are 15-year-old French speakers.)

	Teacher	Student
Errors		
Feedback on errors		
Genuine questions		
Display questions		
Negotiation of meaning		

Photocopiable © Oxford University Press

T OK, we finished the book – we finished in the book Unit 1, 2, 3. Finished Workbook 1, 2, 3. So today we're going to start with Unit 4. Don't take your books yet, don't take your books. In 1, 2, 3 we worked in what tense? What tense did we work on? OK?
S Past
T In the past—What auxiliary in the past?
S Did
T Did (writes on board '1-2-3 Past'). Unit 4, Unit 4, we're going to work in the present, present progressive, present continuous—OK? You don't know what it is?
S Yes
T Yes? What is it?
S Little bit
T A little bit
S ...
T Eh?
S Uh, present continuous
T Present continuous? What's that?
S e-n-g
T i-n-g
S Yes
T What does that mean, present continuous? You don't know? OK, fine. What are you doing, Paul?
S Rien

T Nothing?

S Rien—nothing

T You're not doing anything? You're doing *something*!

S Not doing anything.

T You're doing *something*!

S Not doing anything.

T You're doing *something*—Are, are you listening to me? Are you talking with Marc? What are you doing?

S No, no—uh—listen—uh—

T Eh?

S to you

T You're you're listening to me.

S Yes

T Oh—(writes 'What are you doing? I'm listening to you' on the board)

S Je—

T What are you—? You're excited.

S Yes

T You're playing with your eraser—(writes 'I'm playing with my eraser' on the board). Would you close the door please, Bernard? Claude, what is he doing?

S Close the door

T He is closing the door. (writes 'He's closing the door' on the board) What are you doing, Mario?

S Moi, I listen to you.

T You're listening to me.

S Yes

T OK. Are you sleeping or are you listening to me?

S I don't—moitié-moitié, half and half.

T Half and half, half sleeping, half listening.

Classroom B: A communicative approach
(Students in this class are 10-year-old French speakers. In this activity, they are telling their teacher and their classmates what 'bugs' them. They have written 'what bugs them' on a card or paper which they hold while speaking.)

	Teacher	Student
Errors		
Feedback on errors		
Genuine questions		
Display questions		
Negotiation of meaning		

Photocopiable © Oxford University Press

S It bugs me when a bee string me.
T Oh, when a bee stings me.
S Stings me.
T Do you get stung often? Does that happen often? The bee stinging many times?
S Yeah.
T Often? (Teacher turns to students who aren't paying attention) OK. Sandra and Benoît, you may begin working on a research project, hey? (Teacher turns her attention back to 'What bugs me')
S It bugs me (inaudible) and my sister put on my clothes.
T Ah! She—borrows your clothes? When you're older, you may appreciate it because you can switch clothes, maybe. (Teacher turns to check another student's written work) Mélanie, this is yours, I will check.—OK. It's good.
S It bugs me when I'm sick and my brother doesn't help me— my—my brother, 'cause he—me—
T OK. You know—when (inaudible) sick, you're sick at home in bed and you say, oh, to your brother or your sister: 'Would you please get me a drink of water?'—'Ah! Drop dead!' you know, 'Go play in the traffic!' You know, it's not very nice. Martin!
S It bug me to have—
T It bugs me. It bugzz me
S It bugs me when my brother takes my bicycle. Every day.
T Every day? Ah! Doesn't your bro—(inaudible) his bicycle? Could his brother lend his bicycle? Uh, your brother doesn't have a bicycle?
S Yeah! A new bicycle (inaudible) bicycle.
T Ah, well. Talk to your mom and dad about it. Maybe negotiate a new bicycle for your brother.
S (inaudible)
T He has a new bicycle. But his brother needs a new one too.
S Yes!
T Hey, whoa, just a minute! Jean?

S Martin's brother has—
T Martin, who has a new bicycle? You or your brother?
S My brother.
T And you have an old one.
S (inaudible)
T And your brother takes your old one?
S —clutch—(inaudible) bicycle
T His bicycle! Ah! How old is your brother?
S March 23.
T His birthday?
S Yeah!
T And how old was he?
S Fourteen.
T Fourteen. Well, why don't you tell your brother that when he takes your bike you will take his bike. And he may have more scratches than he figures for. OK?

Characteristics of input in the two classrooms

Classroom A

1 Errors: Very few on the part of the teacher. However the teacher's speech does have some peculiar characteristics typical of this type of teaching, for example, the questions in statement form—often asked with dramatic rising intonation (for example, 'You don't know what it is?'). The students don't make many errors because they don't say very much.

2 Error correction: Yes, constantly from the teacher.

3 Genuine questions: Yes, a few, and they are almost always related to classroom management. No questions from the students.

4 Display questions: Yes, almost all of the teacher's questions are of this type. Interestingly, however, the students sometimes interpret *display questions* as *genuine questions* (T: What are you doing, Paul? S: Rien.)

5 Negotiation of meaning: Very little, learners have no need to paraphrase or request clarifications, and no opportunity to determine the direction of the discourse; the teacher is only focused on the formal aspects of the learners' language.

Classroom B

1 Errors: Yes, when students speak but hardly ever when the teacher does. Nevertheless, the teacher's speech also contains incomplete sentences, simplified ways of speaking, and an informal speech style.

2 Error correction: Yes, sometimes the teacher repeats what the student has said with the correct form (for example, 'he bugzz me'—pointing out the third person singular). However, this correction is not consistent or intrusive as the focus is primarily on letting students express their meanings.

3 Genuine questions: Yes, almost all of the teacher's questions are focused on getting information from the students. The students are not asking questions in this exchange.

4 Display questions: No, because there is a focus on meaning rather than on accuracy in grammatical form.

5 Negotiation of meaning: Yes, from the teacher's side, especially in the long exchange about who has a bicycle!

Summary of the two classroom excerpts

You have no doubt noticed how strikingly different these transcripts from the two classrooms are, even though the activities are both teacher-centred. In the transcript from Classroom A, the focus is on form (i.e. grammar) and in Classroom B, it is on meaning. In Classroom A, the only purpose of the interaction is to practise the present continuous. Although the teacher uses real classroom events and some humour to accomplish this, there is no doubt about what really matters here. There is no real interest in what students 'are doing', but rather in their ability to say it. There is a primary focus on correct grammar, display questions, and error correction in the transcript from Classroom A.

In the transcript from Classroom B, the primary focus is on meaning, conversational interaction, and genuine questions, although there are some brief references to grammatical accuracy when the teacher feels it is necessary.

Five proposals for classroom teaching

The teaching methodologies in Classrooms A and B differ because they reflect opposing theoretical views concerning the most effective way to learn a second language in classroom settings.

Theories have been proposed for the best way to learn a second language in the classroom and teaching methods have been developed to implement them. But the only way to answer the question 'Which theoretical proposal holds the greatest promise for improving language learning in classroom settings?' is through research which specifically investigates relationships between teaching and learning.

Both formal and informal research are needed. Formal research involves careful control of the factors which may affect learning. It often uses large numbers of teachers and learners in order to try to limit the possibility that the unusual behaviour of one or two individuals might create a misleading impression about what one would expect in general. Researchers doing this kind of work must sometimes sacrifice naturalness in order to ensure that only those factors under investigation are different in the groups being compared.

Informal research often involves small numbers, perhaps only one class with one teacher, and the emphasis here is not on what is most general but rather on what is particular about this group or this teacher. While formal research may add strength to theoretical proposals, informal research, including that carried out by teachers in their own classrooms, is also essential. It is hardly necessary to tell experienced teachers that what 'works' in one context may fail in another.

In the section below, we will examine five proposals relating to this issue, provide examples from classroom interaction to illustrate how the proposals get translated into classroom practice, and discuss how the findings from some of the formal research in SLA fit them. For each proposal, a few relevant studies will be presented, discussed, and compared with one another. The labels we have given these proposals are:

1 Get it right from the beginning

2 Say what you mean and mean what you say

3 Just listen

4 Teach what is teachable

5 Get it right in the end

1 *Get it right from the beginning*

The 'Get it right from the beginning' proposal for second language teaching best describes the underlying theory behind the teaching practices observed in Classroom A (page 74). Indeed, it is the proposal which probably best describes the way in which most of us were taught a second language in school. It reflects the behaviourist view of language acquisition in assuming that learners need to build up their language knowledge gradually by practising only correct forms. Teachers avoid letting beginning learners speak freely because this would allow them to make errors. The errors, it is said, could become habits. So it is better to prevent these bad habits before they happen. Here are some more examples from classes based on this approach.

Example 1
(The teacher and students from Classroom A. This time the exercise in based on the simple present of English verbs.)

>   S1 And uh, in the afternoon, uh, I come home and uh, uh, I uh, wash-
>   ing my dog.
>   T   I wash.

S1 My dog.
T   Every day you wash your dog?
S1 No. [ben]
S2 Il n'a pas de chien! (=He doesn't have a dog!)
S1 Non, mais on peut le dire! (=No, but we can say it!)

Clearly, in this case, the student's real experience with his dog (or even the fact that he did or did not have a dog) was irrelevant. What mattered was the correct use of the simple present verb.

Example 2

(A group of 12-year-old learners of English as a foreign language.)

T   Repeat after me. Is there any butter in the refrigerator?
Group Is there any butter in the refrigerator?
T   There's very little, Mom.
Group There's very little, Mom.
T   Are there any tomatoes in the refrigerator?
Group Are there any tomatoes in the refrigerator?
T   There are very few, Mom.
Group There are very few, Mom. (etc.)

Pure repetition. The students have no reason to get involved or to think about what they are saying. Indeed, some students who have no idea what the sentences mean will successfully repeat them anyway, while their minds wander off to other things.

Research findings

There is little classroom research to support this proposal. In fact, it was the frequent failure of traditional grammar-based methods to produce fluency and accuracy in second language learners which led to the development of more communicative approaches to teaching in the first place.

Supporters of communicative language teaching have argued that language is not learned by the gradual accumulation of one item after another. They suggest that errors are a natural and valuable part of the language learning process. Furthermore, they believe that the motivation of learners is often stifled by an insistence on correctness in the earliest stages of second language learning. These opponents of the 'Get it right from the beginning' proposal argue that it is better to encourage learners to develop 'fluency' before 'accuracy'.

Recently, some researchers and educators have reacted to the trend toward communicative language teaching and have revived the concern that allowing learners too much 'freedom' without correction and explicit instruction will lead to early *fossilization* of errors. Once again we hear the call for making sure learners 'get it right from the beginning'.

Unfortunately, little research has been carried out to test the hypothesis that an *early* and *exclusive* emphasis on form will, in the long run, lead to higher levels of linguistic performance and knowledge than an early and exclusive emphasis on meaning. The widespread adoption of communicative language teaching in recent years has meant that researchers in some settings have not been able to find classrooms which are exclusively form-oriented in order to make direct comparisons with classrooms that are exclusively meaning-oriented. None the less, there are findings from second language classroom research which are relevant to this issue. These include descriptive studies of the interlanguage development of second language learners in audiolingual programs (Study 1), and studies of the development of second language proficiency in classroom learners who have received different amounts of form- and meaning-based instruction (Studies 2 and 3).

Study 1: Audiolingual pattern drill

In the late 1970s, Patsy Lightbown and her colleagues in Quebec, Canada, carried out a series of longitudinal and cross-sectional investigations into the effect of audiolingual instruction on the second language interlanguage development of francophone ESL learners, aged eleven to sixteen (Lightbown 1983, 1987). Students in these programs typically participated in the types of rote repetition and *pattern practice drill* we saw in Classroom A on pages 74–5 and 79–80.

The researchers compared aspects of the learners' acquisition of English grammatical morphemes (such as plural -*s* and the progressive -*ing*) with the 'natural' order of acquisition by uninstructed second language learners. The results indicated several differences between the 'natural order' and the order in which these classroom learners produced them. The findings also suggested that the type of instruction provided, a regular diet of isolated pattern practice drills, contributed to the alterations in the learners' natural interlanguage development. For example, while learners were able to produce a particular form (for example, the -*ing* form) with a high degree of accuracy during the time that their instruction focused on it, the same form was produced with considerably less accuracy (and frequency) when it was no longer being practised in class. These findings provided evidence that an exclusive emphasis on accuracy and practice of particular grammatical forms does not mean that learners will be able to use the forms. Not surprisingly, this type of instruction did not seem to favour the development of fluency and communicative abilities either.

Study 2: Grammar plus communicative practice

Sandra Savignon (1972) studied the linguistic and communicative skills of 48 college students enrolled in French language courses at an American university. The students were divided into three groups, all of which received the same number of hours per week of audiolingual instruction where the focus was on the practice and manipulation of grammatical forms. However, the 'communicative group' had an additional hour per week devoted to communicative tasks in an effort to encourage practice in using French in meaningful, creative, and spontaneous ways; the 'cultural group' had an additional hour devoted to activities, conducted in English, which were designed to 'foster an awareness of the French language and culture through films, music and art'; and the *control group* had an additional hour in the language laboratory doing grammar and pronunciation drills similar to those which they did in their regular class periods.

Tests to measure learners' linguistic and communicative abilities were administered before and after instruction to see if there were any significant differences between groups on these measures. The tests of 'linguistic competence' included a variety of grammar tests, teachers' evaluations of speaking skills, and course grades. The tests of 'communicative competence' included measures of fluency and of the ability to understand and transmit information in a variety of tasks, which included: (1) discussion with a native speaker of French, (2) interviewing a native speaker of French, (3) the reporting of facts about oneself or one's recent activities, and (4) a description of ongoing activities.

The results revealed no significant differences between groups on the linguistic competence measures. However, the 'communicative group' scored significantly higher than the other two groups on the four communicative tests developed for the study. Savignon interprets these results as support for the argument that second language programs which focus *only* on accuracy and form do not give students sufficient opportunity to develop communicative abilities in a second language.

Study 3: Grammar plus communicative practice
In a similar study, Carol Montgomery and Miriam Eisenstein (1985) followed a group of adult learners receiving an additional communicative component to their regular, grammar-based instruction. This group was compared to a control group which received only the grammar course. The researchers reported that beginner and intermediate level ESL learners engaging in communicative activities in addition to their regular, required grammar course made greater improvements in accent, vocabulary, grammar, and comprehension than did learners who received only the required grammar course. Somewhat unexpectedly, the area of greatest improvement for the group getting 'real world' communicative practice was in grammatical accuracy.

Interpreting the research

The studies reviewed above provide evidence to support the intuitions of teachers and learners that the 'Get it right from the beginning' proposal is not a very effective way to provide second language instruction. Learners receiving audiolingual instruction or more traditional grammar-based approaches have not benefited from this instruction in a way that permits them to communicate their messages and intentions effectively in a second language. Experience has also shown that primarily or exclusively grammar-based approaches to teaching do *not* guarantee that learners develop high levels of accuracy and linguistic knowledge. In fact, it is often very difficult to determine what such learners know about the target language; the classroom emphasis on accuracy usually results in learners who are inhibited and will not 'take chances' in using their knowledge for communication. The results from these studies support the claim that learners require opportunities for communicative practice.

It is important to emphasize that in the Savignon and the Montgomery and Eisenstein studies, all subjects received their regular, grammar-focused instruction and differed only in terms of the presence or absence of an additional communicative practice component. In other words, these studies offer support for the hypothesis that meaning-based instruction is advantageous, *not* that form-based instruction is not. The contributions of communicative practice and grammar-focused instruction will be discussed in more detail in relationship to the 'Teach what is teachable' and 'Get it right in the end' proposals.

2 *Say what you mean and mean what you say*

This is the theoretical view underlying the teacher-student behaviour in the transcript from Classroom B (pages 75–7). Based on the interactionists' hypothesis, advocates of 'Say what you mean and mean what you say' emphasize the necessity for learners to have access to meaningful and comprehensible input through conversational interactions with teachers and other students. They have argued that when learners are given the opportunity to engage in conversations, they are compelled to 'negotiate meaning', that is, to express and clarify their intentions, thoughts, opinions, etc., in a way which permits them to arrive at a mutual understanding. The negotiation, in turn, leads learners to acquire the language forms—the words and the grammatical structures—which carry the meaning.

Negotiation of meaning is accomplished through a variety of modifications which naturally arise in conversational interaction. For example, learners will ask each other or their teacher for clarification, confirmation, repetition, and other kinds of information as they attempt to negotiate meaning. This can be seen in the transcripts from Classroom B.

The claim is that as learners, in interaction with other learners and teachers, work toward a mutual understanding in the negotiation process, language acquisition is facilitated. Advocates of interactionism argue quite simply that learners will learn by 'saying what they mean and meaning what they say' in conversations which encourage them to do so.

Look for cases of negotiation for meaning in the examples below and compare this with the examples given for the 'Get it right from the beginning' proposal.

Example 3
(The teacher and students from Classroom B (pages 75–7). Students are checking answers on a written task.)

    S Me and Josée, we don't have the same as her.
    T That's fine. Yeah, because there'll be different answers.
    S Why... uh, we do that with a partner?
    T Simply so you can consult.

(In Examples 4, 5, and 6, a group of 12-year-old students are discussing with their teacher a questionnaire about their pets.)

Example 4
    S The fish is difficult to wash?
    T Fish is difficult to wash?
    S Yes.
    T Fish... Oh, not so difficult. Fish are difficult to wash?!? What's your uh... [question]?
    S *Do you have an animal?* Yes, I do. *Do you ever feed it?* Yes, r—
    T Do you know what 'feed' means?
    S Ah, no. It's uh...?
    T To give food to it.

Example 5
    T How often do you walk your dog?
    S Never.
    T Why?
    S Because I don't have a dog.

Example 6
    S And what is 'feed'—?
    T Feed? To feed the dog?
    S Yes, but when I don't have a ...
    T If you don't have a dog, you skip the question.

Example 7
(Students from Classroom B, doing a morning warm-up activity.)

    T How are you doing this morning?

S1 I'm mad!
S2 Why?
T   Oh boy. Yeah, why?
S1 Because this morning, my father say no have job this morning—
T   Your father has no more job this morning? Or you have no job?
S1 My father.

How different these examples are from the essentially meaningless interaction often observed in classrooms where communication and form-focus are separated from each other. Such genuine exchanges of information must surely enhance students' motivation to participate in language learning activities.

Research findings

There have been no studies which have *directly* examined the effects of either the number or type of interaction opportunities on second language acquisition. Most of the research has been descriptive in nature, focusing on such issues as: How does negotiation which takes place in classrooms differ from that observed in natural settings? Do task types contribute to different kinds of interactional modifications? How does teacher- versus student-centred instruction contribute to differences in classroom interaction? Some research has examined relationships between modifications in conversational interaction and comprehension. Here are a few studies relevant to the interactionist proposal.

Study 4: Group work and learner language
One of the earliest studies to measure the different types of interaction patterns in second language settings was carried out by Michael Long and his colleagues (1976). In their study, differences in the quantity and quality of student language in group work versus teacher-centred activities were investigated. They found that the students produced not only a greater quantity but also a greater variety of speech in group work than in teacher-centred activities. Not surprisingly, in the teacher-centred activities, the students primarily responded to teachers' questions and rarely initiated speech on their own. In contrast, learner language in group work activity was filled with questions and responses and many more occasions where learners took the initiative to speak spontaneously. In addition, the learner-centred activities led to a much greater variety of language functions (for example, disagreeing, hypothesizing, requesting, clarifying, and defining).

Although this study was small, involving only two pairs of learners and two 40-minute lessons, it was one of the first studies to suggest how opportunities for more group work interaction may be beneficial for second language learning.

Study 5: Learners talking to learners

Patricia Porter examined the language produced by adult learners performing a task in pairs. There were eighteen subjects in the study: twelve non-native speakers of English whose first language was Spanish, and six native English speakers. The non-native speakers were intermediate or advanced learners of English.

Each subject was asked to participate in separate discussions with a speaker from each of the three levels. For example, an intermediate-level speaker had a conversation with another intermediate-level speaker, with an advanced-level speaker, and with a native speaker of English. The investigator wanted to compare the speech of native and non-native speakers in conversations as well as to compare differences across proficiency levels in these conversation pairs.

Learners talked more with other learners than they did with native speakers. Also, learners produced more talk with advanced-level than with intermediate-level partners, partly because the conversations with advanced learners lasted longer. Porter examined the number of grammatical and vocabulary errors and false starts and found that learner speech showed no differences across contexts. That is, intermediate-level learners did not make any more errors with another intermediate-level speaker than they did with an advanced or native speaker. This is a particularly interesting finding because it calls into question the argument that learners need to be exposed to a native-speaking model (i.e. teacher) at all times if we are to ensure that they produce fewer errors.

Overall, Porter concluded that although learners cannot provide each other with the accurate grammatical input that native speakers can, learners can offer each other genuine communicative practice which includes negotiation of meaning. Supporters of the 'Say what you mean and mean what you say' proposal argue that it is precisely this negotiation of meaning which is essential for language acquisition. (See Long and Porter 1985 for discussion of group work.)

Study 6: Interaction and comprehensibility

In one of the few studies which has directly investigated the effects of different input conditions on comprehension, Teresa Pica, Richard Young, and Catherine Doughty (1987) found that modifications in interaction led to higher levels of comprehension than modifications in input. In their study, the sixteen learners were asked to follow instructions and complete a task under either of two different conditions. In the first condition, the students listened to a script read by a native speaker. The script had been simplified in a number of ways to facilitate comprehension. For example, there were repetition and paraphrasing, simple grammatical constructions and vocabulary, and so on. In the second condition, the learners listened to a script which contained the same information, but which had *not* been simplified in any way. Instead, as learners listened to the script being read, they were encouraged to ask questions and seek verbal assistance when they had any difficulty following the directions.

The results indicated that learners who had the opportunity to ask clarification questions, and check their comprehension as they were listening to the instructions, comprehended much more than the students who received a simplified set of instructions to do the task but had no opportunity to interact while completing it.

Study 7: Learner language and proficiency level

George Yule and Doris Macdonald (1990) investigated whether the role that different proficiency-level learners play in two-way communication tasks led to differences in their interactive behaviour. In order to do this they set up a task which required two learners to communicate information about the location of different buildings on a map and the route to get there. One learner, referred to as the 'sender', had a map with a delivery route on it and this speaker's job was to describe the delivery route to the other learner so that he or she could draw the delivery route on an incomplete map.

To determine whether there would be any difference in the nature of the interactions according to the relative proficiency of the 40 adult participants, different types of learners were paired together: one group which consisted of high-proficiency learners in the 'sender' role and low-proficiency learners in the 'receiver' role, and another group with low-proficiency 'senders' paired with high-proficiency 'receivers'.

The results showed that when low-proficiency learners were in the 'sender' role, the interactions were considerably longer and more varied than when high-proficiency learners were the 'senders'. The explanation provided for this was that high-proficiency 'senders' tended to act as if the lower-proficiency 'receiver' had very little importance and contribution to make in the completion of the task. As a result, the lower-proficiency 'receivers' were almost forced to play a very passive role and said very little in order to complete the task. When low-proficiency level learners were in the 'sender' role, however, much more negotiation of meaning and a greater variety of interactions between the two speakers took place. Based on these findings, the researchers argue that teachers should place more advanced students in less dominant roles in paired activities with lower-proficiency-level learners.

Interpreting the research

The research described above (and other related research) investigating the factors which contribute to the quality and quantity of interactions between second language learners has provided some very useful information for teaching. Certainly, the early work of Long and his colleagues and the more recent findings of Porter and Yule and MacDonald have contributed to a better understanding of how to organize group and pair work more effectively in the classroom.

As indicated above, the difficulty with this line of research is that it is based on the not yet fully tested assumption that specific kinds of interactive behaviours lead to more successful second language acquisition. Although the Pica, Young, and Doughty study is important in this regard because it is one of the first to provide support for the claim that specific types of interactive behaviours lead to greater comprehension, more research is needed to directly test the hypothesis that better comprehension leads to more successful acquisition.

3 Just listen

This proposal is based on the assumption that it is not necessary to drill and memorize language forms in order to learn them. However, unlike the interactionists' emphasis on providing opportunities for interaction of the kind we saw in some of the excerpts in the 'Say what you mean and mean what you say' proposal, the emphasis here is on providing comprehensible input through listening and/or reading activities.

Read the classroom example below to get a feel for how this theory of classroom second language learning can be implemented in classroom practice.

Example 8
It is the English period at a primary school in a French-speaking area of New Brunswick, Canada. Students (aged nine to ten) enter the classroom, which looks very much like a miniature language lab, with small carrels arranged around the perimeter of the room. They go to the shelves containing books and audio-cassettes and select the material which they wish to read and listen to during the next 30 minutes. For some of the time the teacher is walking around the classroom, checking that the machines are running smoothly. She does not interact with the students concerning what they are doing. Some of the students are listening with closed eyes; others read actively, pronouncing the words silently. The classroom is almost silent except for the sound of tapes being inserted or removed or chairs scraping as students go to the shelves to select new tapes and books.

'Just listen' is one of the most influential—and most controversial— approaches to second language teaching because it not only holds that second language learners need not drill and practise language in order to learn it, but also that they do not need to speak at all, except to get other people to speak to them. According to this view, it is enough to hear and understand the target language. And, as you saw in the classroom description above, one way to do this is to provide learners with a steady diet of listening and reading comprehension activities with no (or very few) opportunities to speak or interact with the teacher or other learners in the classroom.

The material which the students read and listen to is not graded in any rigid way according to a sequence of linguistic simplicity. Rather, the program planners grade materials on the basis of what they consider intuitively to be at an appropriate level for the different groups of learners, because a given text has shorter sentences, clearer illustrations, or is based on a theme or topic that is familiar to the learners.

As noted in Chapter 2, the individual whose name is most closely associated with this proposal is Stephen Krashen, particularly with his hypothesis that the crucial requirement for second language acquisition is the availability of comprehensible input.

Research findings

Several studies which are relevant to this proposal include: (1) research in experimental *comprehension-based* ESL programs in Canada; (2) research investigating the effects of the 'Total physical response' method of second language teaching; and (3) research in Canadian French immersion programs.

Study 8: Comprehension-based instruction for children

Example 8 was a description of a real program which was developed in experimental classes in a French-speaking region in Canada. From the beginning of their instruction in grade 3 (age eight years), these francophone students only listen and read during their daily 30-minute ESL period. There is no oral practice or interaction in English at all. Teachers do not 'teach' but provide organizational and technical support. Thus, learners receive a steady diet of native-speaker input but virtually no interaction with the teacher or other learners.

Patsy Lightbown and Randall Halter have investigated the second language development of hundreds of children in this program and have compared these findings with the second language development of those in the regular, aural-oral ESL program at the same grade level. Their results have revealed that learners in the comprehension-based program learn English as well as (and in some cases better than) learners in the regular program (Lightbown 1992). This is true not only for their comprehension skills but also for their speaking skills. This comes as something of a surprise since the learners in the innovative programs *never* practise spoken English in their classes.

Study 9: Total physical response

One of the best-known examples of the 'Just listen' proposal is the second language teaching approach called 'Total physical response' (TPR). In TPR classes, students—children or adults—participate in activities in which they hear a series of commands in the target language, for example: 'stand up', 'sit down', 'pick up the book', 'put the book on the table', 'walk to the door'. For a substantial number of hours of instruction, students are not required to say anything. They simply listen and show their comprehension by their actions. This instruction differs from the comprehension-based instruction described in Study 8 and from Krashen's theoretical version of 'Just listen' in an important way: the vocabulary and structures which learners are exposed to are carefully graded and organized so that learners deal with material which gradually increases in complexity and each new lesson builds on the ones before.

TPR was developed by James Asher, whose research has shown that students can develop quite advanced levels of comprehension in the language without engaging in oral practice (Asher 1972). When students begin to speak, they take over the role of the teacher and give commands as well as following them. It is clear that there are limitations on the kind of language students can learn in such an environment. Nevertheless, the evidence seems to show that, for beginners, this kind of active involvement gives learners a good start. It allows them to build up a considerable knowledge of the language without feeling the nervousness that often accompanies the first attempts to speak the new language.

Study 10: *French immersion programs in Canada*

Other research which is often cited as relevant to the 'Just listen' proposal comes from Canadian French immersion programs, which have been described by Krashen as communicative language teaching 'par excellence'. The reason for this is that the focus in French immersion is on meaning through subject-matter instruction and the provision of rich, comprehensible input. In many ways, Krashen could not have asked for a better laboratory to test his theory. What have the studies shown?

First, there is little doubt that the overall findings provide convincing evidence that these programs are among the most successful large-scale second language programs in existence. Learners develop fluency, functional abilities, and confidence in using their second language. There is, however, a growing awareness that French immersion learners still fail to achieve high levels of performance in some aspects of French grammar even after several years in these programs (Harley and Swain 1984). There are several possible explanations for this.

Some researchers believe that the learners engage in too little language production because the classes are largely teacher-centred and students are not required to give extended answers (Swain 1985). This permits students to operate successfully with their incomplete knowledge of the language because they are rarely pushed to be more precise or more accurate. Communication between students and between teacher and students is quite satisfactory in spite of numerous errors in the students' speech.

Other observers have suggested that the students need more *form-focused* instruction. This is based partly on experimental studies in which the addition of form-focused instruction has been shown to benefit learners (see Studies 14–17 under the 'Get it right in the end' proposal, pages 97–102). It has also been observed that certain linguistic features rarely or never appear in the language of the teacher or the students in these *content-based* instructional environments. Furthermore, the presence in the classroom of other learners whose interlanguages are influenced by the same first language, the same learning environment, and the same limited contact with the target language outside the classroom, make it difficult for an individual learner to work out how his or her own use of the language differs from the target language.

Interpreting the research

The results of the French immersion research confirm the importance of comprehensible input in that the students develop not only good comprehension (in reading and listening), but also confidence and fluency in French. However, research does not support the argument that an exclusive focus on meaning and comprehensible input is enough to bring learners to mastery levels of performance in their second language. Indeed, the fact that French immersion learners continue to make the same linguistic errors after years of exposure to the second language in classrooms which provide a great deal of comprehensible input is a challenge to the claim that language will take care of itself as long as meaningful comprehensible input is provided.

The results of the research on comprehension-based ESL also appear to provide support for Krashen's comprehensible input hypothesis. It is important to keep in mind, however, that the learners in the comprehension-based studies are *beginner-level* learners and it is far too early to know how their second language skills will continue to develop. It is certainly possible (indeed probable) that learners in comprehension-based programs, like the French immersion learners, will have considerable gaps in their linguistic knowledge and performance over time. And, like the French immersion learners, they too will probably need and benefit from opportunities to use the language interactively as well as from some careful form-focused intervention later in their development.

The TPR results also show great benefits for learners in the early stages of development. Krashen says of TPR that it prepares learners to go out into the target language community to get *more* comprehensible input which, he says, will carry their language acquisition further.

In summary, comprehension-based programs appear to be beneficial in the development of basic comprehension and communicative performance in the early stages of learning (particularly in situations where learners have no other contact with the target language apart from in classroom situations). But they may not be sufficient in getting learners to continue to develop their second language abilities to advanced levels.

4 *Teach what is teachable*

The proposal referred to as 'Teach what is teachable' is one which has received increasing attention in second language acquisition research in recent years. The researcher most closely associated with this view is Manfred Pienemann. He and his associates are concerned with being able to explain why it often seems that some things can be taught successfully whereas other things, even after extensive or intensive teaching, seem to remain unacquired. They claim that their research provides evidence that some linguistic structures, for example, basic sentence word order (both simple and complex) develops along a particular developmental path. Thus, for example, any attempt to teach a word order pattern that is a 'Stage 4' pattern to learners at 'Stage 1' will not work because learners have to pass through 'Stage 2' and get to 'Stage 3' before they are ready to acquire what is at 'Stage 4'. The underlying cause of the stages has not been fully explained, but there has been considerable research showing that they may be based at least in part on learners' developing ability to process (unconsciously analyse and organize) certain elements in the stream of speech they hear.

Researchers supporting this view also claim that certain other aspects of language—vocabulary, some grammatical features—can be taught at any time. A learner's success in learning these *variational features* will depend on factors such as motivation, intelligence, and the quality of instruction.

While this line of research has the potential to inform classroom teachers about which aspects of language acquisition are 'developmental' (and thus teachable only in a given sequence) and which are 'variational' (and thus teachable at various points in learner language development), there is much work to be done before the findings of this research can lead to recommendations about whether particular forms can be taught and when.

In Examples 9 and 10 below, we see a teacher trying to help students with question formation. The students seem to know what they mean, but the level of language the teacher is offering them is beyond their current stage of development. A look back at Chapter 4 (pages 63–5) will show you how far the students are from where the teacher would like them to be. The students react by simply answering the question or accepting the teacher's formulation.

Example 9
(A group of twelve-year-old students, interviewing each other as they play the roles of imaginary people.)

    S1 What's your nationality?

S2 I am Greek.

S1 What old, um, do you, uh, have—?

T 'How old' dear. 'How old' were you—?

S1 How old do you have. . . No, never mind.

T How old were you when you came here?

S1 Uh, yeah.

Example 10

(The same group of students, asking fellow students questions about an award poster which they had recently received.)

S1 Mylène, where you put your 'Kid of the Week' poster?

T Where *did* you put your poster when you got it?

S2 In my room.

(2 minutes later)

S3 Mélanie, where you put your 'Kid of the Week' poster?

T Where *did* you put your poster?

S4 My poster was on my wall and it fell down.

In Example 11 below, the student is using a 'fronting' strategy which is typical of Stage 3 learners. That is, the student simply places an auxiliary verb (in this case 'is') at the beginning of the sentence but does not change the rest of the sentence. (Note that if the student had fronted 'does', the sentence would have been correct, but we would not have been able to see how the student thought question formation worked.) In this case, the teacher's correction leads the student to produce a Stage 4 question. In Example 12, the same situation appears. This time, however, the correction leads not to a reformulation of the question, but simply to an answer.

Example 11

(Examples 11, 12, 13, and 14 are from a group of twelve-year-old French speakers learning English as a foreign language.)

('Famous person' interviews)

S1 Is your mother play piano?

T 'Is your mother play piano?'? OK. Well, can you say 'Is your mother play piano?' or 'Is your mother a piano player?'?

S1 'Is your mother a piano player?'

S2 No.

Example 12

(interviewing each other about house preferences)

S1 Is your favourite house is a split-level?

S2 Yes.

T You're saying 'is' two times dear. 'Is your favourite house a split-level?'

S1 A split-level.

T OK.

Example 13
('Hide and seek' game)

    S Where the teacher books are?
    T Where are the teacher's books?
    S Where are the tea—the teacher books?

Here the student asks a Stage 3 question, the teacher provides a Stage 4 correction, and the student is able to make the change. Note, however, that the student still doesn't change the possessive *'s*, something which French speakers find very difficult.

Research findings

The 'Teach what is teachable' view is one which claims that while some features of the language can be taught successfully at various points in the learner's development, other features develop according to the learner's internal schedule, and that no amount of instruction can change the 'natural' developmental course. Let us examine a few of the studies which have tested this hypothesis.

Study 11: Ready to learn

In a study of the acquisition of German as a second language, Manfred Pienemann (1988) investigated whether instruction permitted learners to 'skip' a stage in the natural sequence of development. Two groups of learners who were at Stage 2 in their acquisition of German word order were taught the rules associated with Stage 3 and Stage 4 respectively. The instruction took place over two weeks and during this time, learners were provided with explicit grammatical rules and exercises for Stage 4 constructions. The results showed that the learners who received instruction on Stage 3 rules moved easily into this stage from Stage 2. However, those learners who received instruction on Stage 4 rules did not move into this stage. They either continued to use Stage 2 behaviours or they moved into Stage 3. That is, they were not able to 'skip' a stage in the 'natural route'. Pienemann interprets his results as support for the hypothesis that for some linguistic structures, learners cannot be taught what they are not 'developmentally ready' to learn.

Study 12: Teaching when the time is right

Catherine Doughty (1991) examined whether particular aspects of relative clause formation would benefit from instruction at a time when learners were developmentally 'ready' to learn them. Twenty subjects were divided into three groups: two experimental and one control. All groups received exposure to relative clauses over a period of ten days through a series of computer-delivered reading lessons. During these lessons all learners were asked to read the passages and answer a variety of comprehension questions which focused on reading skills such as skimming and scanning.

For the experimental groups, two instructional techniques were added to the reading comprehension exercises. These were presented to the learners by means of an additional 'window' on the learners' computer screens. One experimental group received instruction which focused on meaning-orientated techniques. This included both vocabulary help and paraphrases of sentences in the reading comprehension texts. The other experimental group received instruction which focused on rules. This included instruction on relative clause formation through a combination of explicit grammatical rules and on-screen sentence manipulation.

All learners were pre-tested immediately before the instructional treatment and post-tested after the ten days of the exposure/instruction with regard to relative clauses.

The results revealed a clear advantage for the experimental groups. That is, learners who had received the additional instruction in relative clause formation—regardless of whether it was meaning-orientated or rule-orientated—outperformed the control group learners who had received only exposure to relative clauses through the reading comprehension texts. Doughty concludes that instruction on relative clauses made a difference when it was provided at the time when learners were 'developmentally ready' to learn them.

Study 13: Can question forms be taught?

Rod Ellis (1984) studied the effects of instruction on the acquisition of question forms by thirteen child ESL learners. In this study, learners were also given instruction at a time when they were considered to be 'developmentally ready' to acquire *wh*-question inversion rules. The learners received three hours of instruction. In the first hour the teacher asked a series of *wh*-questions while referring to a wall poster, and students were asked to respond. In the second hour, the students asked questions (again referring to the wall poster), and the teacher corrected them when they made errors. In the third hour, the teacher 'fired questions at the pupils' about the wall poster. The group results revealed little effect for instruction on the learners' development of question forms, although some individual learners did improve substantially.

Interpreting the research

The conflicting results of these studies present an obvious problem for assessing the 'Teach what is teachable' proposal. A closer look at some of the procedural problems in one of the studies should shed some light on these seemingly contradictory findings. If one compares the amount of instruction provided, it seems possible that the three hours provided in the Ellis study were not enough to cause changes in the learners' interlanguage systems. Further, there is the possibility that the type of instruction was not sufficiently form-focused. In the limited description of the type of instruction provided in Ellis' study, it seems that the learners had more exposure to *wh*-questions in the teacher's modelling than they did opportunities to produce questions themselves and to receive feedback on their errors, either through correction and/or explicit rule teaching. In this way, the group in Ellis' study may have been more similar to the control group in Doughty's study—the one which received increased 'exposure' but not so much 'instruction' and in the end did not perform as well as those learners who received more focused instruction.

It seems reasonable to conclude that because the instruction provided in the Doughty and Pienemann studies was more explicit, carefully controlled, and of a longer duration, their studies provide a more reliable test of the 'Teach what is teachable' proposal. Nonetheless, it is important to note some of the weaknesses in these studies as well. For example, in Doughty's study, no direct comparison was made between learners who were *not* 'developmentally ready' to learn relative clauses and those who *were*. Further, in both studies, only the short-term effects of instruction were measured. Because of this, there is no way of knowing whether instruction had any permanent or long-term effects on the learners' developing interlanguage systems. In Pienemann's study, results were reported for only a small group of learners. In later studies, however, similar results were reported with other learners.

5 *Get it right in the end*

'Get it right in the end' is similar to the 'Teach what is teachable' proposal. Its proponents recognize a role for instruction, but also assume that not everything has to be taught. That is, they assume that much will be acquired naturally, through the use of language for communication. They also agree that some things cannot be taught if the timing of the teaching fails to take the student's readiness (stage of development) into account. This proposal differs from the 'Teach what is teachable' proposal, however, in that it emphasizes the idea that some aspects of language *must* be taught. For example, when an error learners make is the result of transfer from their first language, and when all the learners in a group tend to make the same error, it will be virtually impossible for learners to discover this error on their own. We can see this in Example14, where francophone learners of English are having difficulties with adverb placement.

'Get it right in the end' also differs from 'Just listen' in that it is assumed that learners will need some guidance in learning some specific features of the target language. Furthermore, it is assumed that what learners learn when they are focusing on language itself *can* lead to changes in their interlanguage systems, not just to an appearance of change brought about by conscious attention to a few details of form. On the other hand, the supporters of this proposal do not claim that teaching particular language points will prevent learners from making errors. Nor do they assume that learners will be able to begin using a form or structure with complete accuracy as soon as it is taught. Furthermore, they do not argue that the focused teaching must be done in a way which involves explicit *explanations* of the point or that learners need to be able to *explain* why something is right or wrong. Rather, they claim that the learners' attention must be *focused on* the fact that their language use differs from that of a more proficient speaker. As we will see in the examples below, teachers must look for the right moment to create increased awareness on the part of the learner—ideally, at a time when the learner is motivated to say something and wants to say it as clearly and correctly as possible.

Proponents of 'Get it right in the end' argue that it is sometimes necessary to draw learners' attention to their errors and to focus on certain linguistic (vocabulary or grammar) points. The difference between this proposal and the 'Get it right from the beginning' proposal is that it acknowledges that it is appropriate for learners to engage in meaningful language use from the very beginning of their exposure to the second language. They assume that much of language acquisition will develop naturally out of such language use, without formal instruction which focuses on the language itself.

The difference between this proposal and the 'Just listen' and 'Say what you mean and mean what you say' proposals is that it is not assumed that comprehensible input and meaningful interaction will be enough to bring learners to high levels of accuracy as well as fluency. Researchers who support this proposal argue that learners can benefit from, and sometimes require, explicit focus on the language.

Example 14
(Examples 14, 15, and 16 are taken from a classroom where a group of twelve-year-olds are learning English. In Example 14, they are engaged in an activity where scrambled sentences are re-ordered to form sensible ones. The following sentence has been placed on the board: 'Sometimes my mother makes good cakes.')

    T   Another place to put our adverb?
    S1 After *makes?*
    T   After *makes.*
    S2 Before *good?*
    T   *My mother makes sometimes good cakes.*
    S3 No.
    T   No, we can't do that. It sounds yucky.
    S3 Yucky!
    T   Disgusting. Horrible. Right?
    S4 Horrible!

This is hardly a typical grammar lesson! And yet the students' attention is being drawn to an error virtually all of them (native speakers of French) make in English.

Example 15
(The students are practising following instructions; one student instructs, others colour.)

   S1   Make her shoes brown.
   T   Now, *her* shoes. Are those Mom's shoes or Dad's shoes?
   S2   Mom's.
   T   Mom's. How do you know it's Mom's?
   S1   Because it's *her* shoes.

French speaking learners of English have difficulty with *his* and *her* because French possessives use the grammatical gender of the object possessed rather than the natural gender of the possessor in selecting the appropriate possessive form. The teacher is aware of this and—briefly, without interrupting the activity—helps the learners 'notice' the correct form.

Example 16
(The students are playing 'hide and seek' with a doll in a doll's house, asking questions until they find out where 'George' is hiding.)

   S1   Is George is, is in the living room?
   T   You said 'is' two times dear. Listen to you—you said 'Is George is in—?'. Look on the board. 'Is George in the' and then you say the name of the room.
   S1   Is George in the living room?
   T   Yeah.
   S1   I win!

Note that the teacher's brief correction does not distract the student from his pleasure in the game, demonstrating that focus on form does not have to be meaningless or preclude genuine interaction.

Research findings

In recent years, there has been an increasing interest in examining issues related to this proposal, leading to both descriptive (Study 14) and experimental studies (Studies 15, 16, and 17). Some of the research is described below.

Study 14: Attention to form in communicative ESL
Nina Spada (1987) examined the effects of differences in instruction on the English language proficiency of 48 adult learners enrolled in a six-week intensive course. All learners received communicative instruction, that is, instruction which focused primarily on meaning-based practice and opportunities to use the second language in creative and spontaneous ways. However, some teachers focused more on grammar than others. For

example, the teacher in Class A spent considerably more time teaching grammar than did the teachers in Classes B and C. In Class B, the students' attention was frequently drawn to specific linguistic features, but this was done while students were engaged in communicative activities, not as a separate lesson. In Class C, attention was rarely, if ever, drawn to specific linguistic features.

The learners were given a number of proficiency tests before and after instruction. This included: (1) a listening comprehension test; (2) a reading comprehension test; (3) an oral interview/interaction task; (4) a multiple choice grammar test; (5) a multiple choice discourse test; and (6) a sociolinguistic test.

The results showed that learners in Class A (the ones who received more grammatical instruction) performed slightly better on the grammar test than learners in Classes B and C. Furthermore, the results indicated that learners in Class A improved on some of the other measures as well (listening, speaking, and discourse tests). It was particularly interesting to note that learners in Class B performed best on the oral interview/interaction task. In this class, students were often encouraged to pay attention to the formal aspects of their speech while they were engaged in communicative practice. Spada concluded that instruction which focuses primarily on meaning (i.e. is communication-based) but allows for a focus on grammar within meaningful contexts, works best.

Study 15: Form-focus experiments in ESL

In Quebec, we have investigated the effects of form-focused instruction and corrective feedback on the development of specific linguistic structures in the English of francophone students participating in intensive ESL programs.

According to the findings of a large-scale, descriptive study involving almost 1,000 students in 33 classes, these programs can be considered to be essentially communicative. That is, the emphasis of the teaching is on activities which focus on meaning rather than form, opportunities for spontaneous interaction and the provision of rich and varied comprehensible input. Although learners develop high levels of fluency and communicative ability in their target language, they still have problems with linguistic accuracy and complexity (Spada and Lightbown 1989; Lightbown and Spada 1990).

The experimental studies involved a smaller number of classes. In these studies, the effects of form-focused instruction and corrective feedback on two particular linguistic features were examined: adverb placement and question formation. In the first study, Lydia White (1991) selected adverb placement for investigation because English and French differ with regard to the positions in which adverbs can be placed in sentences. The hypothesis was that learners would persist in using adverb placement rules from French if they were not explicitly told how rules for adverb placement differ in English and French. Questions were selected for the second study because they have been extensively investigated in the literature and considerable comparison data are available, particularly with regard to acquisition sequences.

Both the experimental and the comparison groups were tested before the experiment began (pre-test), and both groups were tested again when the period of special instruction had ended (post-test). The experimental groups received approximately eight hours of instruction over a two-week period. This included explicit teaching of the grammatical rules associated with each structure as well as corrective feedback. The teachers of the experimental groups were provided with a package of teaching materials and a clear set of procedures to follow. The comparison group teachers were asked to teach a different structure, one which was not the focus of the experiment, so that the comparison group learners would be familiar with the tasks and activities that were used in the testing procedures. The studies included immediate, delayed, and long-term/follow-up post-tests. For the adverb study the test tasks were written, and in the question formation study the tests included both written and oral tasks.

The results of the adverb study revealed that learners who received instruction on adverb placement dramatically outperformed the learners who did not receive instruction on adverbs. This was found to be the case on all tests in both the immediate and delayed post-tests (immediately following instruction and six weeks later). In the follow-up tests a year later, however, the gains made by the learners who had received the adverb instruction had disappeared and their performance on this structure was like that of uninstructed learners.

The results of the question formation study revealed that the instructed group made significantly greater gains than the uninstructed group on the written tasks immediately following instruction. Furthermore, it was found that the instructed learners maintained their level of knowledge on later testing (six weeks and six months after instruction). It was also found that a focus on form contributed to improvements in oral performance on questions.

Analysis of classroom language showed that adverbs were very, very rare in classroom speech, giving learners little opportunity to maintain their newly acquired knowledge through continued exposure and use. In contrast, there were hundreds of opportunities to hear and use questions every day in the classroom.

Study 16: Focusing on past tense forms in French immersion
As mentioned earlier in this chapter, there is a growing belief that learners in French immersion programs need more opportunities to focus on form and receive corrective feedback. There has been a call for more classroom

research of the type exemplified by Studies 16 and 17 to determine how this can best be accomplished.

Birgit Harley (1989) examined the effects of a functional approach to grammar teaching on a particularly problematic area of grammar for English-speaking learners of French—the contrastive use of two past tense forms: *imparfait* (roughly, the habitual or descriptive past, for example 'Ma mère *parlait* souvent de son enfance' [My mother often spoke about her childhood]), and *passé composé* (roughly the specific or narrative past, for example, 'Après le cours *j'ai parlé* avec les autres élèves' [After class I talked with the other students]).

Approximately 300 grade 6 immersion students were given instruction on the use of these past tense forms through teaching materials which encouraged their use in a variety of functionally-based practice activities. No explicit grammatical rules were provided, nor was there an emphasis on corrective feedback. The intention was to create opportunities, activities, and tasks which would expose them to more input containing both verb forms, and encourage more productive use of them by the learners. The teaching materials were administered over an eight-week period. Learners were tested on their spoken and written knowledge of the *imparfait* and *passé composé* before the instructional treatment began, eight weeks later, and again three months later.

Harley's findings showed that learners in the experimental classes outperformed the control classes on the immediate post-tests on some of the written and oral measures. Three months later, however, there were no significant differences between the two groups.

Study 17: Focus on the conditional in French immersion
Elaine Day and Stan Shapson (1991) examined the effects of instruction with 315 grade 7 students (age about twelve or thirteen) in French immersion. The feature of French grammar which was taught was the conditional mood of the verb, for example in sentences such as 'Si je gagnais la loterie, je *partirais* en voyage.' [If I won the lottery, I would go away on a trip.]

Students in the experimental classes received several hours of focused instruction on the conditional over a period of five to seven weeks. The students in the control group continued with their usual classroom routines, that is, they continued to encounter French mainly in the context of learning their general school subjects (science, mathematics, history, etc. through the medium of French).

Special teaching materials were prepared by the team of researchers. They consisted of: (1) group work which created situations for the use of the conditional in natural communicative situations; (2) written and oral exercises to reinforce the use of the conditional in more formal, structured situations;

and (3) self-evaluation activities to encourage students to develop conscious awareness of their language use. Oral and written tests were administered before the instructional treatment, immediately after the instruction (five to seven weeks later), and at the end of the school year.

Learners in the experimental classes outperformed those in the control classes on the immediate post-tests for the written tasks (but not for the oral). In contrast to the students in Study 16, they were still doing better than the control group on the follow-up post-tests administered several months later.

Interpreting the research

The overall results of the experimental studies in the intensive ESL and French immersion programs provide partial support for the hypothesis that *enhanced input* or form-focused instruction and corrective feedback within communicative second language programs can improve the learners' use of particular grammatical features. The results also show, however, that the effects of instruction are not always long lasting. For example, in the intensive program studies, the positive effects of form-focused instruction on adverb placement had disappeared a year later. Yet, the positive effects of this type of instruction and corrective feedback for questions were maintained in the long-term follow-up testing. Similarly, in the experimental French immersion studies, while there were only short-term instructional benefits for the use of the *imparfait* and *passé composé*, the benefits of instruction for the use of the conditional continued to be evident several months later.

Enhancing the input

The different results of the intensive ESL program findings might be explained in terms of the frequency of use of the two linguistic structures in regular classroom input after the experimental treatment had ended. For example, as mentioned in Study 15, question forms occur much more frequently in classroom input than adverbs. This continued reinforcement may have contributed to the continued improvement in the learners' use of questions over time. Evidence from classroom observations suggests that students did not receive any continued reinforcement through exposure to adverbs in classroom materials and activities once the experimental period was over, and thus it should not be surprising that these learners failed to maintain the improved performance levels.

The contrasting results of the French immersion program teaching experiments (Studies 16 and 17) may also be explained by potential differences in input. But in this case, it seems more likely that differences in the experimental teaching materials and methodology may have contributed to the different results. Although both sets of materials had as their goal to provide learners with the opportunity to use the linguistic forms in a variety of functionally-based communicative practice activities, the instructional materials for the 'past tense' study (16) may not have been sufficiently form-focused or did not draw the learners' attention to their language use as frequently and as explicitly as the instructional materials for the 'conditional' study (17). While this is a possible explanation, other factors may have contributed to the different outcomes. For example, it could be that the two linguistic structures under investigation respond to instruction in different ways or that even the relatively small differences in the age of the learners played a role.

The implications of classroom research for teaching

It is difficult to draw firm conclusions about the strength of the theoretical proposals until further research is completed. But it is possible to speculate on the 'strongest contenders' on the basis of the classroom research findings so far.

There is increasing evidence that learners continue to have difficulty with basic structures of the language in programs which offer no form-focused instruction. This calls into question the 'Just listen' proposal, which in its strongest form not only claims *no* benefit from form-focused instruction and correction, but suggests that it can actually interfere with second language development. However, we do not find support for the argument that if second language learners are simply exposed to comprehensible input, language acquisition will take care of itself.

There are similar problems with the 'Say what you mean and mean what you say' proposal. As noted earlier in this chapter, there is evidence that opportunities for learners to engage in conversational interactions in group and paired activities can lead to increased fluency and the ability to manage conversations more effectively in a second language. However, the research also shows that learners in programs based on the 'Say what you mean and mean what you say' proposal continue to have difficulty with accuracy as well.

Because these programs emphasize meaning and attempt to simulate 'natural' communication in conversational interaction, the students' focus is naturally on *what* they say, not *how* to say it. This can result in a situation where learners provide each other with input which is often incorrect and incomplete. Furthermore, even when attempts are made to draw the learners' attention to form and accuracy in such contexts (either by the teacher or other learners), these attempted corrections may be interpreted by the learners as continuations of the conversation. Thus, programs based on the 'Just listen' and 'Say what you mean and mean what you say' proposals are incomplete in that learners' gains in fluency and conversational skills may not be matched by their development of accuracy.

It is important to emphasize that the evidence to support a role for form-focused instruction and corrective feedback does not provide support for the 'Get it right from the beginning' proposal. Research has demonstrated that learners *do* benefit considerably from instruction which is meaning-based. The results of the French immersion and intensive ESL program research are strong indicators that many learners develop higher levels of fluency through exclusively or primarily meaning-based instruction than through rigidly grammar-based instruction. The problem remains, however, that certain aspects of the linguistic knowledge and performance of second language learners are not fully developed in such programs.

Unfortunately, research investigating the 'Teach what is teachable' proposal is not yet at a point where it is possible to say to teachers: 'Here is a list of linguistic features which you can teach at any time and here is another list which shows the order in which another set of features will be acquired. You should teach them in this order.' The number of features which researchers have investigated with experimental studies within this framework is simply far too small.

Similarly, second language researchers working from the 'Get it right in the end' proposal cannot yet provide a list of those forms which *must* be taught. Nonetheless, because these proposals do not argue for exclusively form-based or meaning-based instruction, but rather acknowledge a role for form-focused instruction and correction within a communicative program, the 'Teach what is teachable' and 'Get it right in the end' proposals appear to be the most promising at the moment in terms of guiding decisions about second language teaching.

Summary

Classroom data from a number of studies offer support for the view that form-focused instruction and corrective feedback provided within the context of a communicative program are more effective in promoting second language learning than programs which are limited to an exclusive emphasis on accuracy on the one hand or an exclusive emphasis on fluency on the other. Thus, we would argue that second language teachers can (and should) provide guided, form-based instruction and correction in specific circumstances. For example, teachers should not hesitate to correct persistent errors which learners seem not to notice without focused attention. Teachers should be especially aware of errors that the majority of learners in a class are making when they share the same first language background. Nor should they hesitate to point out how a particular structure in a learner's first language differs from the target language. Teachers might also try to become more aware of those structures which they sense are just beginning to emerge in the second language development of their students and provide some guided instruction in the use of these forms at precisely that moment to see if any gains are made. It may be useful to encourage learners to take part in the process by creating activities which draw the learners' attention to forms they use in communicative practice, by developing contexts in which they can provide each other with feedback and by encouraging them to ask questions about language forms.

Decisions about when and how to provide form focus must take into account differences in learner characteristics, of course. Quite different approaches would be appropriate for, say, a trained linguist learning a fourth or fifth language, a young child beginning his or her schooling in a second language environment, an immigrant who cannot read and write his or her own language, and an adolescent learning a foreign language at school.

It could be argued that many teachers are quite aware of the need to balance form-focus and meaning-focus, and that recommendations based on research may simply mean that SLA research has confirmed current classroom practice. Although this may be true to some extent, it is hardly the case that all teachers approach their task with a clear sense of how best to accomplish their goal. It is not always easy to step back from familiar practices and say, 'I wonder if this is really the most effective way to go about this?' Furthermore, many teachers are reluctant to try out classroom practices which go against the prevailing trends among their colleagues or in their educational contexts, and there is no doubt that many teachers still work in environments where there is an emphasis on accuracy which virtually excludes spontaneous language use in the classroom. At the same time, there is evidence that the introduction of communicative language teaching methods has sometimes resulted in a complete rejection of attention to form and error correction in second language teaching.

Teachers and researchers do not face a choice between form-based and meaning-based instruction. Rather, our challenge is to determine which features of language will respond best to form-focused instruction, and which will be acquired without explicit focus if learners have adequate exposure to the language. In addition, we need to develop a better understanding of how form-based instruction can be most effectively incorporated into a communicative framework. Continued classroom-centred research in second language teaching and learning should provide us with insights into these and other important issues in second language learning in the classroom.

Sources and suggestions for further reading

An overview of language teaching approaches

Richards, J. and T. Rodgers. 1986. *Approaches and Methods in Language Teaching*. Cambridge: Cambridge University Press.

Get it right from the beginning

Hammerly, H. 1987. 'The immersion approach: Litmus test of second-language acquisition through classroom communication.' *Modern Language Journal* 71: 395–401.

Higgs, T. V. and R. Clifford. 1982. 'The push toward communication' in T. V. Higgs (ed.): *Curriculum, Competence, and the Foreign Language Teacher*. Skokie, Ill.: National Textbook Co. pp. 57–79.

Lado, R. 1964. *Language Teaching: A Scientific Approach*. New York: McGraw-Hill.

Study 1: Audiolingual programs in Quebec

Lightbown, P. M. 1983. 'Acquiring English L2 in Quebec classrooms' in S. Felix and H. Wode (eds.): *Language Development at the Crossroads*. Tübingen: Gunter Narr. pp. 151–75.

Lightbown, P. M. 1987. 'Classroom language as input to second language acquisition' in C. Pfaff (ed.): *First and Second Language Acquisition Processes*. Cambridge, Mass.: Newbury House. pp. 169–87.

Study 2: Grammar plus communicative practice

Savignon, S. 1972. *Communicative Competence: An Experiment in Foreign-language Teaching*. Philadelphia, Pa.: Center for Curriculum Development.

Study 3: Grammar plus communicative practice

Montgomery, C. and **M. Eisenstein.** 1985. 'Reality revisited: An experimental communicative course in ESL.' *TESOL Quarterly* 19: 317–34.

Say what you mean and mean what you say

Gass, S. and **E. Varonis.** 1985. 'Task variation and nonnative/nonnative negotiation of meaning' in S. Gass and C. Madden (eds.): *Input in Second Language Acquisition*. Rowley, Mass.: Newbury House. pp. 149–61.

Hatch, E. 1978. 'Discourse analysis and second language acquisition' in E. Hatch (ed.): *Second Language Acquisition: A Book of Readings*. Rowley, Mass.: Newbury House. pp. 401–35.

Study 4: Group work and learner language

Long, M. H., L. Adams, M. McLean, and **F. Castanos.** 1976. 'Doing things with words—verbal interaction in lockstep and small group classroom situations' in J. Fanselow and R. Crymes (eds.): *On TESOL '76*. Washington, D.C.: TESOL. pp. 137–53.

Study 5: Learners talking to learners

Long, M. and **P. Porter.** 1985. 'Group work, interlanguage talk, and second language acquisition'. *TESOL Quarterly* 19: 207–28.

Study 6: Interaction and comprehensibility

Pica, T., R. Young, and **C. Doughty.** 1987. 'The impact of interaction on comprehension'. *TESOL Quarterly* 21: 737–59.

Study 7: *Learner language and proficiency level*

Yule, G. and **D. Macdonald.** 1990. 'Resolving referential conflicts in L2 interaction: The effect of proficiency and interactive role.' *Language Learning* 40: 539–56.

Just listen

Krashen, S. 1982. *Principles and Practice in Second Language Acquisition.* Oxford: Pergamon.

Krashen, S. 1985. *The Input Hypothesis: Issues and Implications.* London: Longman.

Study 8: *Comprehension-based instruction for children*

Lightbown, P. M. 1992. 'Can they do it themselves? A comprehension-based ESL course for young children' in R. Courchêne, J. Glidden, J. St. John, and C. Thérien (eds.): *Comprehension-based Second Language Teaching/L'Enseignement des langues secondes axé sur la compréhension.* Ottawa: University of Ottawa Press. pp. 353–70.

Study 9: *Total physical response*

Asher, J. 1972. 'Children's first language as a model for second language learning.' *Modern Language Journal* 56: 133–9.

Study 10: *French immersion programs in Canada*

Harley, B. and **M. Swain.** 1984. 'The interlanguage of immersion students and its implications for second language teaching' in A. Davies, C. Criper, and A. Howatt (eds.): *Interlanguage.* Edinburgh: Edinburgh University Press. pp. 291–311.

Swain, M. 1985. 'Communicative competence: Some roles of comprehensible input and comprehensible output in its development' in S. Gass and C. Madden (eds.): *Input in Second Language Acquisition.* Rowley, Mass.: Newbury House.

Teach what is teachable

Pienemann, M. 1985. 'Learnability and syllabus construction' in K. Hyltenstam and M. Pienemann (eds.): *Modelling and Assessing Second Language Acquisition.* Clevedon, UK: Multilingual Matters. pp. 23–75.

Pienemann, M., M. Johnston, and **G. Brindley.** 1988. 'Constructing an acquisition-based procedure for second language assessment.' *Studies in Second Language Acquisition* 10: 217–43.

Study 11: *Ready to learn*

Pienemann, M. 1988. 'Determining the influence of instruction on L2 speech processing.' *AILA Review* 5: 40–72.

Study 12: Teaching when the time is right

Doughty, C. 1991. 'Second language instruction does make a difference: Evidence from an empirical study of SL relativization.' *Studies in Second Language Acquisition* 13/4: 431–69.

Study 13: Can question forms be taught?

Ellis, R. 1984. 'Can syntax be taught?' *Applied Linguistics* 5: 138–55.

Get it right in the end

Lightbown, P. M. 1991. 'What have we here? Some observations on the role of instruction in second language acquisition' in R. Phillipson, E. Kellerman, L. Selinker, M. Sharwood-Smith, and M. Swain (eds.): *Foreign/Second Language Pedagogy Research: A Commemorative Volume for Claus Færch*. Clevedon, UK: Multilingual Matters.

Long, M. H. 1991. 'Focus on form: A design feature in language teaching methodology' in K. de Bot, D. Coste, R. Ginsberg, and C. Kramsch (eds.): *Foreign Language Research in Cross-cultural Perspective* Amsterdam: John Benjamins. pp. 39–52.

Rutherford, W. 1987. 'The meaning of grammatical consciousness-raising.' *World Englishes* 6: 209–16.

Sharwood Smith, M. 1991. 'Speaking to many minds: On the relevance of different types of language information for the L2 learner.' *Second Language Research* 7: 118–32.

White, L. 1987. 'Against comprehensible input: The input hypothesis and the development of second-language competence.' *Applied Linguistics* 8: 95–110.

Study 14: Attention to form in communicative ESL

Spada, N. 1987. 'Relationships between instructional differences and learning outcomes: A process-product study of communicative language teaching.' *Applied Linguistics* 8: 137–61.

Study 15: Form-focus experiments in ESL

Spada, N. and P. M. Lightbown. 1989. 'Intensive ESL programs in Quebec primary schools.' *TESL Canada Journal* 7: 11–32.

Spada, N. and P. M. Lightbown. 1993. 'Instruction and the development of questions in L2 classrooms.' *Studies in Second Language Acquisition* 15/2.

White, L. 1991. 'Adverb placement in second language acquisition: some effects of positive and negative evidence in the classroom.' *Second Language Research* 7: 133–61.

White, L., N. Spada, P. M. Lightbown, and **L. Ranta.** 1991. 'Input enhancement and syntactic accuracy in L2 acquisition.' *Applied Linguistics* 12: 416–32.

Study 16: Focusing on past tense forms in French immersion

Harley, B. 1989. 'Functional grammar in French immersion: A classroom experiment.' *Applied Linguistics* 10: 331–59.

Study 17: Focus on the conditional in French immersion

Day, E. and **S. Shapson.** 1991. 'Integrating formal and functional approaches to language teaching in French immersion: An experimental approach.' *Language Learning* 41: 25–58.

6 POPULAR IDEAS ABOUT LANGUAGE LEARNING: FACTS AND OPINIONS

In the Introduction, we presented a number of commonly expressed opinions about how languages are learned and what the implications are for how they should be taught. We asked you to indicate how strongly you agreed with these opinions. Now that you have read about some of the theory and research in second language acquisition, take another look at those opinions. Have you changed your mind about the importance of imitation or groupwork, or whether starting second language instruction early is really the best approach? Or do you feel that your intuitions about SLA have only been confirmed by the discussion in the preceding chapters?

To conclude this introduction to SLA research, we present our own responses to these popular ideas about language learning.

1 Languages are learned mainly through imitation

It is difficult to find support for the argument that languages are learned mainly through imitation when one thinks of the countless examples of novel utterances that language learners produce. This is particularly evident with children who say things like: 'I'm hiccing up and I can't stop' and 'It was upside down but I turned it upside right'. These examples and many others included in Chapter 1 provide evidence that language learners create their own system of rules through the development of hypotheses about how language works.

This does not mean, however, that imitation has no role to play in language learning. Some learners, particularly children learning their first language, imitate a great deal. Yet their language does not develop faster or better than that of children who rarely imitate. Furthermore, as we saw in Chapter 1, children do not imitate everything they hear, but often selectively imitate certain words or structures which they are in the process of learning. This is also true of younger and older learners learning their second language in natural settings.

2 Parents usually correct young children when they make grammatical errors

There is considerable variation in the extent to which parents correct their children's speech. Nevertheless, the research based on extensive observations of parents and children shows that parents tend to focus on meaning rather than form when they correct their children's speech. Thus, they may correct an incorrect word or an incorrect statement of the facts, but errors which do not interfere with successful communication are rarely corrected.

3 People with high IQs are good language learners

In classroom settings where the emphasis is on learning *about* the language (for example, grammar rules and vocabulary items), learners with superior intelligence tend to do well—as they do in other academic subjects. However, in classrooms where language acquisition through interactive language use is emphasized, research has shown that learners with a wide variety of intellectual abilities can be successful language learners.

4 The most important factor in second language acquisition success is motivation

Everyone agrees that learners who want to learn tend to do better than those who don't. But we must guard against too strong an interpretation of this. There are several things to keep in mind:

1 There are differences in language learning aptitude, and sometimes even highly motivated learners encounter great difficulties in improving their mastery of the language. We know, for example, that learners who begin learning as adults rarely achieve the easy fluency and accuracy that child learners eventually achieve. This should not be taken as evidence that they do not want to learn the language.

2 Research findings suggest a circular cause and effect relationship between motivation and success in second language learning. That is, the more one succeeds, the greater one's motivation; the greater one's motivation, the more one succeeds.

3 Classroom teachers can develop positive motivation in their students by making the classroom itself an environment in which students experience success. This, in turn, can contribute to positive motivation, leading to still greater success.

5 The earlier a second language is introduced in school programs, the greater the likelihood of success in learning

The decision about when to introduce second language instruction must depend on the objectives of the language program in the particular social context of the school. When the objective is native-like or near native-like performance in the second language, then it is desirable to begin exposure to the language as early as possible.

In the case of children from minority language backgrounds or homes where language, literacy, and education are not well-developed, an early emphasis on the second language (the language of the majority) may lead to academic and personal problems. For these children, programs promoting the development of the first language at home and at school may be necessary.

When the objective is basic communicative ability for all students, in a context where there is a strong commitment to maintaining and developing the child's native language, it may be more efficient to begin second language teaching later. Older children are able to catch up very quickly to those who began earlier.

Any school program should be based on realistic estimates of how long it takes to learn a second language. One or two hours a week—even for seven or eight years—will not produce very advanced second language speakers.

6 Most of the mistakes which second language learners make are due to interference from their first language

There are many causes for errors in learner language. The transfer of patterns from the native language is one cause, but more significant is overgeneralization of the target language rules. Learners from different language backgrounds make the same errors when learning a particular second language.

One thing which is very clear is that second language learning is not simply a process of putting second language words into first language sentences. Furthermore, aspects of the second language which are different from the first language will not necessarily be acquired later or with more difficulty than aspects which are similar.

On the other hand, when errors are caused by the overextension of some partial similarity between the first and second languages, the errors may be especially hard to overcome—particularly if learners are frequently in contact with other learners who make the same errors.

7 Teachers should present grammatical rules one at a time, and learners should practise examples of each one before going on to another

Language learning is not linear in its development. Learners may use a particular form accurately at stage X in their development (suggesting that they have learned that form), fail to produce that form correctly at stage Y, and produce it accurately again at stage Z. This usually happens when learners are incorporating new information about the language into their own internal system of rules. An example of this would be when learners who have learned the past tense form 'went' as a memorized 'chunk' learn to use the regular *-ed* inflection for past tense marking. At this point, they stop using 'went' and produce 'goed'. Once the learners become aware of the exceptions to the *-ed* past tense rule, they begin to use 'went' correctly again. This reflects the fact that language development is not just adding rule after rule, but integrating new rules into the existing system of rules, re-adjusting and restructuring until all the pieces fit.

8 Teachers should teach simple language structures before complex ones

Researchers have shown that, no matter how the language is presented to learners, certain structures are acquired before others. This suggests that it is neither necessary nor desirable to restrict learners' exposure to certain linguistic structures which are perceived by a linguist as being 'simple'.

On the other hand, as pointed out in Chapter 5, there is ample evidence to show that when native speakers or fluent bilinguals address a second language learner, they quite naturally adapt their speech to ensure that the learner understands them. This modified speech contains a wide variety of linguistic structures, but tends to leave out complex forms. Teachers, like parents, intuitively increase the complexity of their language as the learner's proficiency increases.

Nevertheless, teachers working in immersion programs, subject-matter second language programs, and communicative language teaching should be aware that some linguistic forms are so rare in their everyday speech that learners have very little opportunity to hear, use, and learn them if the teacher does not make a point of providing them. These need not be difficult or complex forms, however. For example, in the study carried out in intensive communicative ESL classes in Quebec (see Chapter 5, page 103), teachers almost never used adverbs!

9 Learners' errors should be corrected as soon as they are made in order to prevent the formation of bad habits

Errors are a natural part of language learning. This is true of the development of a child's first language as well as of second language learning by children and adults. The errors reveal the patterns of learners' developing interlanguage systems—showing where they have overgeneralized a second language rule or where they have inappropriately transferred a first language rule to the second language.

When errors are persistent, especially when they are shared by almost all students in a class, it is useful to bring the problem to the learners' attention. This does not mean learners should be expected to adopt the correct form or structure immediately or consistently. If the error is based on a developmental pattern, the correction may only be useful when the learner is ready for it. It may thus require many repetitions.

Excessive error correction can have a strong negative effect on motivation. On the other hand, teachers have a responsibility to help learners do their best, and this sometimes means drawing their attention to persistent errors or to errors for which communicative language interaction does not provide natural sources of correction.

10 Teachers should use materials that expose students only to language structures which they have already been taught

Such a procedure can provide comprehensible input, of course, but—given a meaningful context—learners can comprehend the general meaning of many forms which they certainly have not 'mastered' and, indeed, may never have produced. Thus, restricting classroom second language materials to those which contain little or nothing which is new may have several negative consequences:

1 There will soon be a loss of motivation if students are not challenged.

2 Students need to learn to deal with 'real' or 'authentic' material. They do this at first with the teacher's guidance, then independently. Restricting them to step-by-step exposure to the language extends their dependency.

3 Learners who successfully acquire English outside classrooms certainly are exposed to a variety of forms and structures which they have not mastered.

When a particular point is introduced for the first time or when the teacher feels there is a need for correction of a persistent problem, it is appropriate to use narrow-focus materials which isolate one element in a context where other things seem easy. But it would be a disservice to students to use such materials exclusively or even predominantly.

11 When learners are allowed to interact freely (for example, in group or pair activities), they learn each others' mistakes

As reported in Chapter 5, some research has shown that second language learners do not produce any more errors in their speech when talking to learners at similar levels of proficiency than they do when speaking to learners at more advanced levels or to native speakers. Research has also shown that second language learners can provide each other with corrective feedback in group work interaction if this is carefully planned and learners are made aware of the need for accuracy practice within the context of their communicative group work.

Group work is a valuable addition to the variety of activities which encourage and promote second language development. Used in combination with individual work and teacher-centred activities, it plays an important role in communicative language teaching.

12 Students learn what they are taught

It is certainly true that second language learners can only learn the language they are exposed to. However, it certainly is not the case that students learn everything they are taught or that they eventually know only what they are taught. As we have seen, some teaching methods (especially audio-lingual instruction) sometimes give learners the opportunity to learn only a very restricted number of words and sentence types. Even when the language teaching method provides much richer language input, the fact that something is taught or made available in the input does not mean learners will acquire it right away. For example, we have seen that researchers have shown that some aspects of the second language develop according to 'natural' sequences of development.

Attempts to teach things which are too far away from the learner's current stage of development will usually be frustrating. Thus, for learning to be successful, the material which is taught must be appropriate for the learner's stage of development. Other aspects of language, for example, vocabulary, can be taught at any time, as long as the learners are interested in the opportunity to learn and the teaching methods are appropriate to the learner's age, interests, and learning styles. Fortunately, research has also shown that learners learn a great deal that no one ever teaches them. They are able to use their own internal learning mechanisms to discover many of the complex rules and relationships which underlie the language they wish to learn. Students, in this sense, may be said to learn much more than they are taught.

Conclusion

Knowing more about second language acquisition research will not tell you what to do in your classroom tomorrow morning. We hope, however, that this book has provided you with information which has encouraged you to reflect on your experience in teaching. We hope, in addition, that this reflection will contribute to a better understanding of your responsibilities as a teacher and those of your students as language learners.

As we have seen, language learning is affected by many factors. Among these are the personal characteristics of the learner, the structure of the native and target languages, opportunities for interaction with speakers of the target language, and access to correction and form-focused instruction. It is clear that teachers do not have control over all these factors. However, a better understanding of them will permit teachers and learners to make the most of the time they spend together in the twin processes of teaching and learning a second language.

GLOSSARY

We have included in this glossary only those items which have a special or technical meaning in second language acquisition research and second language teaching. The definitions are intended to reflect the terms *as we use them* in this book. Other writers may give different interpretations to some of them. As a rule, we have not included words for which definitions can readily be found in a dictionary (for example, interlocutor, empirical).

accuracy order: The relative accuracy of grammatical forms in learner language. For example, learners are often more accurate in using plural -*s* than in using possessive -'*s*. Some researchers have inferred that accuracy order is equivalent to sequence of acquisition.

audiolingual approach: Audiolingual teaching is based on the behaviourist theory of learning and on structural linguistics. This instructional approach emphasizes the formation of habits through the practice, memorization, and repetition of grammatical structures in isolation from each other and from contexts of meaningful use.

behaviourism: A psychological theory that all learning, whether verbal or non-verbal, takes place through the establishment of habits. According to this view, when learners imitate and repeat the language they hear in their surrounding environment and are positively reinforced for doing so, habit formation (or learning) occurs.

caretaker talk: See *modified input.*

cognitive maturity: The ability to engage in problem solving, deduction, and complex memory tasks.

cognitive theory: A psychological theory which views learning as the building up of knowledge systems which can eventually be called on automatically for speaking and understanding.

communicative competence: The ability to use language in a variety of settings, taking into account relationships between speakers and differences in situations. The term has sometimes been interpreted as the ability to convey messages in spite of a lack of grammatical accuracy.

communicative language teaching (CLT): CLT is based on the premise that successful language learning involves not only a knowlege of the structures and forms of a language, but also the functions and purposes that a language serves in different communicative settings. This approach to teaching emphasizes the communication of meaning over the practice and manipulation of grammatical forms.

comprehensible input: A term introduced by Stephen Krashen to refer to language which a learner can understand. The language may be comprehensible in this sense through the aid of clues such as gestures, situations, or prior information.

comprehension-based instruction: A general term to describe a variety of second language programs in which the focus of instruction is on comprehension rather than production (for example, Total Physical Response).

content-based instruction: Second language programs in which lessons are organized around topics, themes, and/or subject matter rather than language points (for example, French *immersion programs*).

contrastive analysis hypothesis (CAH): The CAH predicts that where there are similarities between the first and second languages, the learner will acquire second language structures with ease; where there are differences, the learner will have difficulty.

control group: In experimental studies, a group of learners which, ideally, differs from the experimental group only in terms of a single factor which is manipulated by the researcher. Performance of the control group is used to show that the factor in question is the best (or only) explanation for changes in the experimental group.

corrective feedback: An indication to a learner that his or her use of the target language is incorrect. This includes a variety of responses that a language learner receives. Corrective feedback can be explicit (for example, 'No, you should say "goes", not "go"') or implicit (for example, 'Yes, he *goes* to school every day'), and may or may not include metalinguistic information (for example, 'Don't forget to make the verb agree with the subject').

correlation: A statistical procedure which compares the frequency or size of different factors in order to determine whether there is a relationship between the two. For example, if students with the highest grades in French also spend the greatest number of hours doing their homework, this would be a positive correlation. It is important to keep in mind, however, that correlation does not imply that one of the variables causes the other.

creative construction: A theory that second language acquisition is a process by which a learner constructs his/her own rule system (i.e. internal representations) for the language being learned. These internal representations are thought to develop slowly in the direction of the full second language system in predictable stages. Creative construction emphasizes the similarity of learners from different first language backgrounds and minimizes the importance of *transfer*.

critical period hypothesis (CPH): The proposal that there is a specific and limited time period for language acquisition. There are two versions of the CPH. The strong version is that a language must be learned by puberty or it will never be learned from subsequent exposure. The weak version is that language learning will be more difficult and incomplete after puberty.

cross-sectional study: A research method in which subjects at different ages and stages of development are studied. Inferences are sometimes drawn from cross-sectional studies about sequences which would apply to the development of individual learners. This contrasts with *longitudinal studies.*

developmental error: An error in learner language which does not result from *transfer* from the first language, but which reflects the learner's gradual discovery of the second language system. These errors are often similar to those made by children learning the language as their mother tongue.

developmental features: Those aspects of a language which, according to Pienemann and his colleagues, develop in a particular sequence, regardless of input variation or instructional intervention.

developmental sequences: The order in which certain features of a language (for example, *grammatical morphemes*) are acquired in language learning.

display question: A question to which the asker already knows the answer. Teachers often ask these questions (for example, 'What color is your shirt?') not because they are genuinely interested in the answer, but rather, to get the learner to display his or her knowledge of the language.

enhanced input: additional, *form-focused instruction* and *corrective feedback* in communicative language programs.

ESL: English as a Second Language. This refers to the learning of English for use in a setting where English is the principal language used (for example, immigrants learning English in Britain).

first language (mother tongue, native language): The language first learned. Many children learn more than one language from birth and may be said to have more than one mother tongue. The abbreviation *L1* is often used.

foreigner talk: See *modified input.*

formal language learning setting: A setting in which second language learners receive instruction and opportunities to practise. In this context, efforts are made to develop the learner's awareness of how the language system works. Typically, this type of learning takes place in the second language classroom.

form-focused instruction: Instruction which draws attention to the forms and structures of the language within the context of communicative interaction. This may be done by giving metalinguistic information, simply highlighting the form in question, or by providing *corrective feedback.*

formulaic patterns or routines: These are expressions which are learned as unanalysed wholes or 'chunks' (for example, 'How old are you?').

fossilization: A lack of change in *interlanguage* patterns, even after extended exposure to or instruction in the target language.

genuine question: In contrast to *display questions,* genuine questions are asked when there is a focus on information: the asker does not know the answer in advance (for example, 'What did you do at the weekend?').

grammaticality judgement: A type of task/test in which subjects are asked to give their view about whether a sentence is correct or incorrect. In some cases, learners are also asked to correct those sentences they judge to be incorrect.

grammatical morphemes: The smallest units of language that carry meaning (for example, *'s* in 'Paul's book' to indicate possession).

immersion program: Programs in which a second language is taught via *content-based instruction.* That is, students study subjects such as mathematics and social studies in their second language. In these programs, little time is spent focusing on the formal aspects of the second language. Typically, students in immersion programs all share the same first language.

informal language learning setting: A setting in which the second language is not taught, but rather, is learned naturally, i.e. 'on the job' or 'in the streets', through informal conversations and interactions with native speakers of the language being learned.

innatism: A theory that human beings are born with some basic knowledge about languages in general that makes it possible to learn the specific language of the environment.

input: The language which the learner is exposed to (either written or spoken) in the environment.

interactionism: A theory that language acquisition is based both on learners' innate abilities and on opportunities to engage in conversations in which other speakers modify their speech to match the learners' communication requirements.

interlanguage: The learner's developing second language knowledge. It may have characteristics of the learner's native language, characteristics of the second language, and some characteristics which seem to be very general and tend to occur in all or most interlanguage systems. Interlanguages are systematic, but they are also dynamic, continually evolving as learners receive more input and revise their hypotheses about the second language.

L1: See *first language.*

L2: See *second language* and *target language.*

language acquisition: This term is most often used interchangeably with *language learning.* However, for some researchers, most notably Stephen Krashen, acquisition is contrasted with learning. Acquisition is thought to represent 'unconscious' learning, which takes place when the emphasis is on communication and there is no attention to form.

language acquisition device (LAD): A metaphor for the innate knowledge of the 'universal' principles common to all human languages. The presence of this knowledge permits children to discover the structure of a given language on the basis of a relatively small amount of input.

language learning: In this book, this term is a general one which simply refers to a learner's developing knowledge of the target language. In Stephen Krashen's terms, however, 'learning' is contrasted with 'acquisition', and is described as a 'conscious' process which occurs when the learner's objective is to learn about the language itself, rather than to understand messages which are conveyed through the language.

longitudinal study: A study in which the same learners are studied over a period of time. This contrasts with *cross-sectional studies.*

meaning-based instruction: See *communicative language teaching.*

metalinguistic awareness: The ability to treat language as an object, for example, being able to define a word, or to say what sounds make up that word.

modified input: Adapted speech which adults use to address children and native speakers use to address language learners so that the learner will be able to understand. Examples of modified input include shorter, simpler sentences, slower rate of speech, and basic vocabulary.

modified interaction: Adapted conversation patterns which native speakers use in addressing language learners so that the learner will be able to understand. Examples of interactional modifications include comprehension checks, clarification requests, and self-repetitions.

morpheme: See *grammatical morpheme.*

native-like: The ability to comprehend and produce a second language at a level of performance which is hardly distinguishable from that of a *native speaker.*

native speaker: A person who has learned a language from an early age and who has full mastery of that language. Native speakers may differ in terms of vocabulary and stylistic aspects of language use, but they tend to agree on the basic grammar of the language.

natural order: See *developmental sequences.*

negotiation of meaning: Interaction between speakers who make adjustments to their speech and use other techniques in order to facilitate communication. See also *modified interaction.*

obligatory contexts: The place in a sentence where a particular grammatical form is required if the sentence is to be correct. For example, in the sentence 'Yesterday, my brother rent a car', the speaker has created an obligatory context for the past tense by the use of 'yesterday', but has not correctly supplied the required form of the verb.

order of acquisition: See *developmental sequences.*

overgeneralization error: This type of error is the result of trying to use a rule in a context where it does not belong, for example, a regular *-ed* ending on an irregular verb.

pattern practice drill: An audiolingual teaching technique in which learners are asked to practise sentences chosen to represent particular linguistic forms.

rate of development: The speed at which learners progress in their language development.

second language: Any language other than the first language learned. The abbreviation *L2* is often used.

simplification: Leaving out elements of a sentence, for example when all verbs have the same form regardless of person, number, tense, for example, 'I go today. He go yesterday.').

structural grading: A technique for organizing or sequencing material in a textbook or lessons. The basis for the organization is a gradual increase in complexity of grammatical features.

subjects: Participants whose knowledge or performance is observed in a research study.

substitution drill: An audiolingual teaching technique in which learners practise sentences, changing one element at a time, for example, 'I read a book'; 'I read a newspaper'; 'I read a story'.

subtractive bilingualism: This is often the result of learning a second language when one's first language skills are not fully developed. In this situation, the first language is partially or completely lost.

target language: The language which is being learned, whether it is the first language or a second (or third or fourth) language.

teacher talk: See *modified input.*

transfer: Learners' use of patterns of the first language in second language sentences. Also called 'interference'.

Universal Grammar (UG): Children's innate linguistic knowledge which, it is hypothesized, consists of a set of principles common to all languages. This term has replaced the earlier term *language acquisition device* in work based on Chomsky's theory of language acquisition.

variational features: In contrast to the *developmental features* in the framework developed by Pienemann and his colleagues, variational features (for example, vocabulary, some grammatical morphemes) can be learned at any point in the learner's development.

BIBLIOGRAPHY

This list of books and articles is not meant to be an exhaustive bibliography of the field of language learning. Rather, it brings together all the works which have been cited in this book as well as those which have been suggested for further reading.

Asher, J. 1972. 'Children's first language as a model for second language learning.' *Modern Language Journal* 56: 133–9.

Baron, N. 1992. *Growing Up with Language*. Reading, Mass.: Addison-Wesley.

Bloom, L. and **M. Lahey.** 1978. *Language Development and Language Disorders*. New York: John Wiley and Sons.

Brown, R. 1973. *A First Language: The Early Stages*. Cambridge, Mass.: Harvard University Press.

Chomsky, N. 1959. Review of *Verbal Behavior* by B.F. Skinner. *Language* 35: 26–58.

Chomsky, N. 1981. *Lectures on Government and Binding*. Dordrecht: Foris.

Cook, V. 1988. *Chomsky's Universal Grammar*. London: Basil Blackwell.

Cook, V. 1991. *Second Language Learning and Language Teaching*. London: Edward Arnold.

Cummins, J. 1984. *Bilingualism and Special Education: Issues in Assessment and Pedagogy*. Clevedon, UK: Multilingual Matters.

Curtiss, S. 1977. *Genie: A Psycholinguistic Study of a Modern-day 'Wild Child.'* New York: Academic Press.

Day, E. and **S. Shapson.** 1991. 'Integrating formal and functional approaches to language teaching in French immersion: An experimental approach.' *Language Learning* 41: 25–58.

de Villiers, J. G. and **P. A. de Villiers.** 1973. 'A cross-sectional study of the acquisition of grammatical morphemes.' *Journal of Psycholinguistic Research* 2: 267–78.

de Villiers, J. G. and **P. A. de Villiers.** 1978. *Language Acquisition.* Cambridge, Mass.: Harvard University Press.

Doughty, C. 1991. 'Second language instruction does make a difference: Evidence from an empirical study of SL relativization.' *Studies in Second Language Acquisition* 13/4: 431–69.

Dulay, H., M. Burt, and **S. Krashen.** 1982. *Language Two.* Oxford: Oxford University Press.

Ellis, R. 1984. 'Can syntax be taught?' *Applied Linguistics* 5: 138–55.

Ellis, R. 1986. *Understanding Second Language Acquisition.* Oxford: Oxford University Press.

Gardner, R. 1985. *Social Psychology and Second Language Learning: The Role of Attitudes and Motivation.* London: Edward Arnold.

Gass, S. and **E. Varonis.** 1985. 'Task variation and nonnative/nonnative negotiation of meaning' in S. Gass and C. Madden (eds.): *Input in Second Language Acquisition.* Rowley, Mass.: Newbury House. pp. 149–61.

Genesee, F. 1976. 'The role of intelligence in second language learning.' *Language Learning* 26: 267–80.

Guiora, A., B. Beit-Hallahmi, R. Brannon, C. Dull, and **T. Scovel.** 1972. 'The effects of experimentally induced changes in ego states on pronunciation ability in a second language: An exploratory study.' *Comprehensive Psychiatry* 13: 139–50.

Hammerly, H. 1987. 'The immersion approach: Litmus test of second-language acquisition through classroom communication.' *Modern Language Journal* 71: 395–401.

Harley, B. 1989. 'Functional grammar in French immersion: A classroom experiment.' *Applied Linguistics* 10/3: 331–59.

Harley, B. and **M. Swain.** 1984. 'The interlanguage of immersion students and its implications for second language teaching' in A. Davies, C. Criper, and A. Howatt (eds.): *Interlanguage.* Edinburgh: Edinburgh University Press. pp. 291–311.

Hatch, E. 1978. 'Discourse analysis and second language acquisition' in E. Hatch (ed.): *Second Language Acquisition: A Book of Readings.* Rowley, Mass.: Newbury House. pp. 401–35.

Higgs, T.V. and **R. Clifford.** 1982. 'The push toward communication' in T. V. Higgs (ed.): *Curriculum, Competence, and the Foreign Language Teacher.* Skokie, Ill.: National Textbook Co. pp. 57–79.

Ingram, D. 1989. *First Language Acquisition: Method, Description and Explanation.* Cambridge: Cambridge University Press.

Itard, J.-M.-G. 1962. *The Wild Boy of Aveyron (L'Enfant sauvage).* New York: Meredith.

Johnson, J., and **E. Newport.** 1989. 'Critical period effects in second language learning: The influence of maturational state on the acquisition of English as a Second Language.' *Cognitive Psychology* 21: 60–99.

Keenan, E. and **B. Comrie.** 1977. 'Noun phrase accessibility and Universal Grammar.' *Linguistic Inquiry* 8: 63–99.

Krashen, S. 1982. *Principles and Practice in Second Language Acquisition.* Oxford: Pergamon.

Krashen, S. 1985. *The Input Hypothesis: Issues and Implications.* London: Longman.

Lado, R. 1964. *Language Teaching: A Scientific Approach.* New York: McGraw-Hill.

Larsen-Freeman, D. and **M. H. Long.** 1991. *An Introduction to Second Language Acquisition Research.* New York: Longman.

Lightbown, P. M. 1983. 'Acquiring English L2 in Quebec classrooms' in S. Felix and H. Wode (eds.): *Language Development at the Crossroads.* Tübingen: Gunter Narr. pp.151–75.

Lightbown, P. M. 1985. 'Great expectations: Second language acquisition research and classroom teaching.' *Applied Linguistics* 6/2: 173–89.

Lightbown, P. M. 1987. 'Classroom language as input to second language acquisition' in C. Pfaff (ed.): *First and Second Language Acquisition Processes.* Cambridge, Mass.: Newbury House. pp. 169–87.

Lightbown, P. M. 1991. 'What have we here? Some observations on the role of instruction in second language acquisition' in R. Phillipson, E. Kellerman, L. Selinker, M. Sharwood-Smith, and M. Swain (eds.): *Foreign/ Second Language Pedagogy Research: A Commemorative Volume for Claus Færch.* Clevedon, UK: Multilingual Matters.

Lightbown, P. M. 1992. 'Can they do it themselves? A comprehension-based ESL course for young children' in R. Courchêne, J. Glidden, J. St. John, and C. Thérien (eds.): *Comprehension-based Second Language Teaching/L'Enseignement des langues secondes axé sur la compréhension.* Ottawa: University of Ottawa Press. pp. 353–70.

Lightbown, P. M. and **N. Spada.** 1990. 'Focus on form and corrective feedback in communicative language teaching: Effects on second language learning.' *Studies in Second Language Acquisition* 12: 429–48.

Long, M. H. 1985. 'Input and second language acquisition theory' in S. Gass and C. Madden (eds.): *Input in Second Language Acquisition.* Rowley, Mass.: Newbury House. pp. 377–93.

Long, M. H. 1990. 'Maturational constraints on language development.' *Studies in Second Language Acquisition* 12: 251–85.

Long, M. H. 1991. 'Focus on form: A design feature in language teaching methodology' in K. de Bot, D. Coste, R. Ginsberg, and C. Kramsch (eds.): *Foreign Language Research in Cross-cultural Perspective.* Amsterdam: John Benjamins. pp. 39–52.

Long, M. H., L. Adams, M. McLean, and **F. Castanos.** 1976. 'Doing things with words—verbal interaction in lockstep and small group classroom situations' in J. Fanselow and R. Crymes (eds.): *On TESOL '76.* Washington, D.C.: TESOL. pp. 137–53.

Long, M. H. and **P. Porter.** 1985. 'Group work, interlanguage talk, and second language acquisition.' *TESOL Quarterly* 19: 207–28.

McLaughlin, B. 1987. *Theories of Second Language Learning.* London: Edward Arnold.

Meisel, J. M., H. Clahsen, and **M. Pienemann.** 1981. 'On determining developmental stages in natural second language acquisition.' *Studies in Second Language Acquisition* 3: 109–35.

Montgomery, C. and **M. Eisenstein.** 1985. 'Reality revisited: An experimental communicative course in ESL.' *TESOL Quarterly* 19: 317–34.

Newport, E. 1990. 'Maturational constraints on language learning.' *Cognitive Science* 14: 11–28.

Obler, L. 1989. 'Exceptional second language learners' in S. Gass, C. Madden, D. Preston, and L. Selinker (eds.): *Variation in Second Language Acquisition, Vol. II: Psycholinguistic Issues.* Clevedon, UK/Philadelphia, Pa.: Multilingual Matters. pp. 141–59.

Oxford, R. 1990. *Language Learning Strategies: What Every Teacher Should Know.* New York: Newbury House.

Patkowski, M. 1980. 'The sensitive period for the acquisition of syntax in a second language.' *Language Learning* 30/2: 449–72.

Pica, T., R. Young, and **C. Doughty.** 1987. 'The impact of interaction on comprehension.' *TESOL Quarterly* 21: 737–59.

Pienemann, M. 1985. 'Learnability and syllabus construction' in K. Hyltenstam and M. Pienemann (eds.): *Modelling and Assessing Second Language Acquisition.* Clevedon, UK: Multilingual Matters. pp. 23–75.

Pienemann, M. 1988. 'Determining the influence of instruction on L2 speech processing.' *AILA Review* 5: 40–72.

Pienemann, M. 1989. 'Is language teachable? Psycholinguistic experiments and hypotheses.' *Applied Linguistics* 10/1: 52–79.

Pienemann, M., M. Johnston, and **G. Brindley.** 1988. 'Constructing an acquisition-based procedure for second language assessment.' *Studies in Second Language Acquisition* 10: 217–43.

Reid, J. 1987. 'The learning style preferences of ESL students.' *TESOL Quarterly* 21/1: 87–111.

Richards, J. and **T. Rodgers.** 1986. *Approaches and Methods in Language Teaching.* Cambridge: Cambridge University Press.

Rutherford, W. 1987. 'The meaning of grammatical consciousness-raising.' *World Englishes* 6: 209–16.

Rymer, R. 1993. *Genie: An Abused Child's Flight from Silence.* London: Michael Joseph.

Sachs, J., B. Bard, and **M. Johnson.** 1981. 'Language learning with restricted input: Case studies of two hearing children of deaf parents.' *Applied Psycholinguistics* 2: 33–54.

Savignon, S. 1972. *Communicative Competence: An Experiment in Foreign-language Teaching.* Philadelphia, Pa.: Center for Curriculum Development.

Schumann, J. 1979. 'The acquisition of English negation by speakers of Spanish: A review of the literature' in R. W. Andersen (ed.): *The Acquisition and Use of Spanish and English as First and Second Languages.* Washington, DC: TESOL.

Scovel, T. 1988. *A Time to Speak: A Psycholinguistic Inquiry into the Critical Period for Human Speech.* Cambridge, Mass.: Newbury House.

Selinker, L. 1972. 'Interlanguage.' *IRAL* 10: 209–31.

Sharwood Smith, M. 1991. 'Speaking to many minds: On the relevance of different types of language information for the L2 learner.' *Second Language Research* 7: 118–32.

Skehan, P. 1989. *Individual Differences in Second Language Learning.* London: Edward Arnold.

Snow, C. and **M. Hoefnagel-Höhle.** 1978. 'The critical period for language acquisition: Evidence from second language learning.' *Child Development* 49: 1114–28.

Spada, N. 1987. 'Relationships between instructional differences and learning outcomes: A process-product study of communicative language teaching.' *Applied Linguistics* 8/2: 137–61.

Spada, N. and **P. M. Lightbown.** 1989. 'Intensive ESL programs in Quebec primary schools.' *TESL Canada Journal* 7: 11–32.

Spada, N. and **P. M. Lightbown.** 1993. 'Instruction and the development of questions in L2 classrooms.' *Studies in Second Language Acquisition* 15/2.

Swain, M. 1985. 'Communicative competence: Some roles of comprehensible input and comprehensible output in its development' in S. Gass and C. Madden (eds.): *Input in Second Language Acquisition.* Rowley, Mass.: Newbury House.

Wesche, M.B. 1981. 'Language aptitude measures in streaming, matching students with methods, and diagnosis of learning problems' in K. Diller (ed.): *Individual Differences and Universals in Language Learning Aptitude.* Rowley, Mass.: Newbury House. pp. 119–39.

White, L. 1987. 'Against comprehensible input: The input hypothesis and the development of second-language competence.' *Applied Linguistics* 8/2: 95–110.

White, L. 1989. *Universal Grammar and Second Language Acquisition.* Amsterdam/Philadelphia, Pa.: John Benjamins.

White, L. 1991. 'Adverb placement in second language acquisition: Some effects of positive and negative evidence in the classroom.' *Second Language Research* 7: 133–61.

White, L., N. Spada, P. M. Lightbown, and **L. Ranta.** 1991. 'Input enhancement and syntactic accuracy in L2 acquisition.' *Applied Linguistics* 12/4: 416–32.

Wong-Fillmore, L. 1991. 'When learning a second language means losing the first.' *Early Childhood Research Quarterly* 6: 323–46.

Yule, G. and **D. Macdonald.** 1990. 'Resolving referential conflicts in L2 interaction: The effect of proficiency and interactive role.' *Language Learning* 40: 539–56.

INDEX

Entries relate to Chapters 1 to 6 and the glossary. References to the glossary are indicated by 'g' after the page number.

accent 43
accessibility heirarchy 65–6
accuracy order 59, 119g
acquisition *see* language acquisition
acquisition-learning hypothesis 26–7
adolescent learners 46–9
affective filter hypothesis 28–9
age of acquisition 41–50, 112–13
American Sign Language (ASL) 13
aptitude 37–8
ASL *see* American Sign Language
attitudes 39–40
audiolingual approach 73–9, 83, 119g
audiolingual pattern drill 81
auditory discrimination 46
'aural' learners 40

behaviourism 1–7, 23–5, 119g
  see also audiolingual approach; 'get it right
    from the beginning'
bilingualism *see* subtractive bilingualism
biology, basis for innatist position 10–13

CAH *see* contrastive analysis hypothesis
caretaker talk 14–15
  see also modified input
children,
    first languages 1–17, 111–12, 112–13
    second languages 19, 20–2, 41–50
  see also learner language
Chomsky, N. 7–10, 26
clarification requests 30
classroom learning 69–110
CLT *see* communicative language teaching
cognitive development 57
cognitive maturity 21–2, 119g
cognitive theory 25–6, 119g
communicative competence 39, 119g
communicative language teaching (CLT) 29,
    74–8, 119g
communicative practice, v. grammar 81–2
comprehensibility, effect of interaction 86–7

comprehensible input 28, 29–30, 120g
comprehension-based instruction 88–9, 91,
    120g
comprehension checks 30
content-based instruction 91, 120g
  see also immersion programs
contrastive analysis hypothesis (CAH) 23–4,
    54–5, 120g
  see also transfer
control group 82, 120g
corrective feedback 20, 21, 99–100, 120g
correlation 36, 120g
CPH *see* critical period hypothesis
creative construction 26, 120–1g
critical period hypothesis (CPH) 11–13,
    42–50, 121g
cross-sectional studies 58, 121g

deaf signers 13
developmental errors 56, 121g
developmental features 92–6, 121g
developmental sequences 57–67, 121g
  see also rate of development
display questions 73, 77, 78, 121g
drills *see* pattern practice drills; substitution
    drills

enhanced input 99–103, 121g
error analysis 55
errors,
    correction 22, 71, 72, 77, 112, 114–15
    due to interference 55–7, 113
    in learner language 53–68
    prevention 79–80, 114–15
ESL (English as a Second Language) 121g
extroversion 35, 38

feedback *see* corrective feedback
first language 1–17, 121g
    grammatical morphemes 57–8
    negative sentences 59–60
    question formation 61–3

foreigner talk 22
    see also modified input
formal language learning settings 20, 121g
form-focused instruction 72–83, 91,
        97–106, 122g
formulaic patterns 6, 122g
fossilization 80, 122g
fronting, question formation 62, 63, 65,
        93–4

genuine questions 73, 77, 78, 122g
'get it right from the beginning' 79–83, 104,
        106–7
'get it right in the end' 96–103, 105, 109
'good language learners', characteristics 33–5
grammar-based instruction 81–2
grammatically judgement 45–6, 122g
grammatical morphemes 28, 54, 57–9, 81,
        122g
grammatical rules 27–8, 45–6, 95, 113–14
    see also Universal Grammar
group work 85, 115–16

imitation 2, 3, 4, 5, 111
immersion programs 90–2, 100–2, 103,
        122g
immigrants, second language acquisition
        41–2, 43–8, 113
informal language learning settings 19,
        69–73, 122g
inhibition 38
innatism 7–13, 26, 122g
    see also communicative language teaching
input 23, 122g
    see also comprehensible input; modified
        input
input hypothesis 28
instructional settings 69–79
intelligence 36–7, 112
interaction,
    effect on comprehensibility 86–7
    see also modified interaction;
        interactionism; negotiation of meaning
interactionism 13–15, 29–30, 122g
    see also communicative language teaching;
        'say what you mean . . .'
interference *see* transfer
interlanguage 55, 122–3g
IQ *see* intelligence

'just listen' 88–92, 103

Krashen, S. 26–9, 90, 91

L1 *see* first language

L2 *see* second language; target language
LAD *see* language acquisition device
language acquisition 123g
language acquisition device (LAD) 8, 11,
        123g
language acquisition order *see* developmental
        sequences
language learning 123g
    theories 1–17, 19–31
learner characteristics 19–22, 33–52
learner language 53–68
    relation to proficiency level 87
learner profiles 20–1
'learners talking to learners' 86, 115–16
learning conditions 21, 22
learning styles 40–1
longitudinal studies 58, 123g

meaning, *see* communicative language
        teaching; negotiation of meaning
metalinguistic awareness 19, 21–2, 123g
Modern Language Aptitude Test (MLAT)
        37–8
modified input 14–15, 22, 72, 73, 123g
modified interaction 14–15, 29–30, 123g
monitor hypothesis 27
monitor model 26–9
morphemes *see* grammatical morphemes
morphology 46–7
'motherese' 14–15
mother tongue *see* first language
motivation, second language learning 35–6,
        39–40, 112
    see also affective filter hypothesis

native language *see* first language
native-like 34, 123g
native speaker 124g
natural order hypothesis 27–8
    see also developmental sequences
natural settings 69–73
    see also informal language learning settings
negative sentences 59–60
negotiation of meaning 73–8, 83–5, 124g
    see also interaction

obligatory contexts 13, 124g
order of acquisition *see* developmental
        sequences
overgeneralization errors 6, 56, 124g

paraphrase 30
parents, error-correction by 8, 112
pattern practice drills, 81, 124g

Peabody Picture Vocabulary Test 47
personality 38–9
Pimsleur Language Aptitude Battery 37–8
power relationships 40
practice 2, 4, 81–2
proficiency level, relation to learner language
     87
pronouns 9–10
pronunciation 38, 43, 46
puberty, critical period hypothesis 11, 43–9

question formation 61–5, 92–4, 95

rate of development 12, 58, 124g
'ready to learn' 94
reflexive pronouns 9–10
relative clauses 65–6
'restructuring' 25

'say what you mean and mean what you say'
     83–8, 103–4
second language 9, 124g
second language learning,
  in classroom 69–110
  factors affecting 33–52
  grammatical morphemes 58–9
  negative sentences 60
  question formation 64–5
  theories 19–31
  see also settings
self-repetition 30
sentence judgement tasks 47
sentence repetition tasks 47

sentence translation 47
settings *see* formal language learning settings;
     informal language learning settings;
     instructional settings
simplification 56, 124g
SLA (Second Language Acquisition) *see*
     second language learning
social dynamics 40
story comprehension tasks 47
storytelling tasks 47
structural grading 72, 124g
'students learn what they are taught' 116
subjects 38, 44–9, 81–3, 85–7, 89–91,
     94–5, 98–102, 124g
substitution drills 4, 124g
subtractive bilingualism 50, 124g

target language 23, 125g
teacher talk 22
  see also modified input
'teaching when the time is right' 92–3
'teach what is teachable' 92–6, 105
total physical response (TPR) 89–90, 91
transfer 24, 57, 66, 113, 125g
  see also contrastive analysis hypothesis

Universal Grammar (UG) 8, 125g
'untamed' children 11–13

variational features 92, 125g
'visual' learners 40

'wild' children 11–13